From the Eye
OF THE
Storm

From the Eye
OF THE
Storm

✫ ✫ ✫

A PASTOR TO THE PRESIDENT SPEAKS OUT

✫ ✫ ✫

J. Philip Wogaman

Westminster John Knox Press
Louisville, Kentucky

The poem by Dorothy L. Nolte on page 38 is adapted from the book *Children Learn What They Live.* Poem copyright © 1972 by Dorothy Law Nolte. Book copyright © 1998 by Dorothy Law Nolte and Rachel Harris. Used by permission of Workman Publishing Co., Inc., New York. All rights reserved.

The quotation from John C. Bennett on page 111 is from his book *Christians and the State* (New York: Charles Scribner's Sons, 1958), page 296. The quotations from Senator Mark Hatfield on page 119 are from his *Between a Rock and a Hard Place* (Waco, Texas: Word Books, 1976), pages 15–16.

The references in chapter 6 to my own previous writing on virtue in public life is from J. Philip Wogaman, *Christian Perspectives on Politics* (Philadelphia: Fortress Press, 1988), chapter 10. And the song with which the book ends is "Evening Skies" by Evelyn Thompson Towle, in *Adventures in Song* (Delaware, Ohio: Cooperative Song Service, c. 1946), page 82.

Scripture quotations, unless otherwise noted, are from the New Revised Standard Version of the Bible, copyright © 1989 by the Division of Christian Education of the National Council of the Churches of Christ in the U.S.A., and are used by permission.

Book and cover design by PAZ Design Group

First edition
Published by Westminster John Knox Press
Louisville, Kentucky

This book is printed on acid-free paper that meets the American National Standards Institute Z39.48 standard. ♾

PRINTED IN THE UNITED STATES OF AMERICA

98 99 00 01 02 03 04 05 06 07 — 10 9 8 7 6 5 4 3 2 1

ISBN 0-664-22140-8

TO REVEREND TOM FARLEY

*Whose influence on my ministry and that
of many others has been incalculable*

— CONTENTS —

— PREFACE —

This book has been written, almost literally, from "the eye of the storm." I wrote it in the midst of a raging national debate. The immediate issue was whether a president of the United States should be forced from office as a consequence of a sexual scandal and his misleading testimony about it. The possible impeachment or forced resignation of a president is, in itself, a prospect of grave importance. But the debate has ranged beyond the immediate crisis to other highly significant questions that must be addressed by the nation. Some of these issues recur frequently in the life of a democratic nation. Our need to struggle with them is more obvious and more urgent in the face of a great political crisis, but they are issues that a democratic society must consider thoughtfully even when there is no immediate decision to be made.

This book was completed just before the midterm congressional elections of 1998. The results of those elections eased the country's mood of crisis to a considerable extent. In light of that, I was tempted to recast the language of some parts of the book, where the focus is upon a crucial decision yet to be made. But, upon reviewing those parts, it seems to me that the crisis mood in which the book was written helps us focus upon the important questions. Those issues are not just academic ones; they have to do with real life. Perhaps they are best seen and discussed in relation to the actual struggles in which we have been engaged. Before the troubled year 1998 recedes too far from memory, we need to reflect upon what we have learned.

I wrote this book more quickly than any of my previous writings, partly because I have been greatly stirred by the crisis and want to help resolve it in a constructive way. In fact, that work must continue. I am personally involved in the present situation in ways this book will indicate, and I feel it is time to speak out. The book cannot and will not violate any pastoral confidences, but I hope it will contribute perspective to an ongoing national debate.

The immediate question of whether the president should be removed from office forces us to examine the meaning of that office more closely, seeing how it may be similar to but also very different from other positions of leadership in our society. What is the special mandate that comes with election to the highest office in the land, and under what circumstances can and should that mandate be nullified by impeachment? That is the immediate question. The way such a question is resolved cannot fail to affect the whole political structure. In particular, the crisis we have been through forces us to reexamine the role of the presidency.

As a pastor and a longtime professor of ethics, I have focused especially on the moral issues. For instance, there is the question of a public leader's private, personal behavior as it relates to public responsibility and leadership. Clearly, everything about a leader's moral character matters, but are there differences between the more private and more public aspects of that? And, indeed, can we adequately assess anybody's moral character if we focus entirely on a small number of personal virtues or flaws of character? In our time, the public seems to want to know everything about its leaders! That is an altogether understandable desire, but it does raise the question whether there may be aspects of anybody's life— including the chief executive of the land—that should be off-limits to public inquiry. How much should be public, and how much should be private? Where do we draw the line?

The present controversy raises the question whether violation of the law renders a high public official unfit to continue in office. All would agree that some kinds of violation of law clearly disqualify a leader—which is why the Constitution provides for impeachment. But how important are the particular circumstances? Of course, there are many related issues involving the scope and conduct of the Office of Independent Counsel—the special prosecutor—as these have related to the present crisis.

Much of the debate pushes us toward consideration of profound issues of law and morality. These are issues that will be around long after the present crisis has been fully resolved, although the events of this year can give us greater insight for the years to come. I am especially intrigued by the deepest question of all: Do we ultimately define ourselves as a community based on law, or is there a deeper sense in which we are a community of mutual caring? I have addressed that question in this book, but I am sure we will have to continue to face it as long as our nation exists. The reason is that we must take ourselves seriously as a nation in which law is respected and, at the same time, we must be a society in which there are deep bonds of human love. The question is: Which of these, law or love, must give way when they are in conflict? Such a question forces us to reach deeply into the moral, spiritual, and legal traditions that have formed us as a people.

Some of the issues the crisis has brought to our attention are distinctly moral and spiritual. When somebody has done something wrong, what kind of repentance is needed? What forms of healing are required? What kinds of penance or punishment? Are there limits to the forgiveness that is sought and given? Lurking beneath such questions, there is also the realization that nobody is perfect. Just how important should that fact be to us as we assess the sins that are more highly publicized than our own? Does it matter that the nation's culture itself prepares the way for wrongdoing through some of the values it emphasizes? Can we get at "cultural sin" simply by punishing the most visible wrongdoers? What happens to a community when some people are demonized?

Among other questions raised by thoughtful people are those focusing on the role of the media in a society that is increasingly dominated by mass communications. News gatherers and commentators often voice their commitment to truth. But what is truth? Is it simply the accumulation of facts? What is the responsibility of the media in seeking to define reality for the rest of us? How has competition among media outlets contributed to the sensationalizing of the news, with distortion of truth as an inevitable consequence?

The national crisis has led to debate over these and other issues. Such a moment in the life of our nation is difficult, even tragic. It has given rise to much grief. But it is also a time when we can deepen our understandings of what really matters and of recommitting ourselves as a nation to a high conception of our life together as a people.

A book of this kind is not a treatise based upon specific research. It is very unlike most of my previous books on ethics. It is a commentary, based partly upon personal experience, partly on widely shared public information, and partly upon many years of previous study and writing. I have tried to write it in such a way that it can be widely read and understood.

One more thing. The crisis has been a national tragedy. It has caused intense suffering in the lives of people, some of whom I know and love. And it has been a time of sadness and uncertainty for millions of people. I do not think it appropriate to profit by this in any way. Therefore, my family and I have decided that any royalties from this book will be used for charitable causes and not for our personal gain.

I am grateful for secretarial assistance from Sally

Mathews. I also wish to thank my colleague Walter Shropshire, my son Steve, and my wife, Carolyn, for careful reading and criticism of the manuscript, and my editor at Westminster John Knox Press, Stephanie Egnotovich, who devoted enormous energy and insight to the editing process. I must bear full responsibility for any inadequacies in the book, but these people have helped me improve it.

I want also to express special gratitude to the people of Foundry Church. They have responded to a very unusual situation with extraordinary Christian grace. They, and the people of other communities of faith across the land, help point the way toward moral renewal and national reconciliation.

From the Eye
OF THE
Storm

— 1 —

The Gathering Storm

For seven months, the nation had been preoccupied with the continuing White House crisis. By late summer 1998, events appeared to be moving toward a culmination. Monica Lewinsky, the former White House intern who was alleged to have had a sexual relationship with the president, had arrived at an agreement with special prosecutor Kenneth Starr and testified at length before a Washington, D.C., grand jury. The president himself had agreed to offer testimony before the grand jury on August 17. As the date approached, the nation's attention was focused on Washington.

As pastor of Foundry United Methodist Church, the president's and first lady's Washington congregation, I was deeply interested in these events. Nevertheless, while the nation was looking toward Washington, my family and I were in a very different place. We had retreated to our favorite vacation spot by the shores of a small lake in the Adirondack Mountains of northern New York. Lake Eaton is a beautiful place. Its crystal waters are surrounded by forest and mountains. The night sky, after sunset, displays brilliant stars. It is a grand place to lay aside the burdens of the year and be restored by God's creation. We needed that time apart from pastoral pressures and responsibilities.

Always in the back of our minds, even in the peacefulness of the northern woods, was the crisis that had gripped the nation and distracted the government for months. But we weren't thinking as much about it in those days by the lake.

Our peaceful time came to an abrupt end. The Friday before the president's scheduled appearance before the grand jury, a park ranger bicycled up to our campsite with a message. I was to call my secretary as quickly as possible. As quickly as possible meant going out to a pay phone by the highway and managing a conversation over the roar of logging trucks. I had been asked, she reported, to participate in the Reverend Jesse Jackson's television program the following Sunday, August 16. Reverend Jackson wanted me there to comment on the issues developing around President Clinton's forthcoming appearance before the grand jury. I doubt whether he thought I would have anything to contribute on the legal or political issues, but there were moral and religious issues, and the president attends our church. I gave it careful thought. There were, I thought, limits to what I could or should say. Still, there were things I felt I needed to say. The CNN producer of the program would arrange for me to appear through a New York or Massachusetts television station so it would not be necessary to end our vacation, and that sounded fine at first.

But then we thought some more. Carolyn voiced her concern first. "Phil," she said, "we belong back in Washington. This crisis is just too important. It involves too many people we care about." She was right, so we packed up and came home. Reverend Jackson's program, "Both Sides with Jesse Jackson" proceeded conversationally. I was joined in that thirty-minute discussion by my Foundry colleague Dr. Walter Shropshire and by Jesse Jackson himself. It was a pretty compatible discussion. We didn't know what would happen in the president's testimony or what he might say afterwards, but we agreed that this gifted political leader still had much to contribute to the nation. We cited relevant biblical passages and discussed the way God had continued to use morally imperfect people. In fact, it is not too great an exaggeration to say that most of the characters in the Bible, including those who did the most good, were very human and had their share of moral weaknesses.

I respected Reverend Jackson and his TV audience, although I was not sure how wide the program's impact would be. The program was, however, picked up by the Associated Press and widely referred to the next day in newspapers across the country. That, in turn, led to an increasing number of other requests for interviews and comments in the days ahead.

BEING DRAWN IN

Let's be honest about it. Most pastors, myself included, do not exactly shy away from public attention.

It's one of our occupational sins. At the same time we can be a little ambivalent about it. The pastoral instinct is to avoid controversial situations. There are good reasons for that. In the first place, we know we can't be experts on everything. Often, we just haven't had the time or competence to delve into all the factual details. Then, too, we don't want to take sides in partisan controversies where there is bound to be some truth—and some error—on both sides. Perhaps most important of all, we don't want to compromise our pastoral effectiveness by speaking of personal matters in a public way. I have been especially concerned about this in the midst of the present political environment. When people share things in confidence with a pastor, the confidentiality must be respected. The way we speak or write of our pastoral responsibilities should strengthen, not weaken, the trust of those who hear or read what we have to say. Everybody should feel that they can pour out their hearts to their pastors or priests or rabbis, knowing that it will stay right there. That is as true of prominent parishioners as it is of anyone else. The only exceptions should be when maintaining silence presents a danger to somebody (such as a situation of child or spousal abuse) or when the person wishes to have something known by others. Even such exceptions have to be handled very carefully. Pastoral privacy is so important that it is respected by law in almost all states and the District of Columbia. A pastor cannot be required to testify in court concerning confidences shared in such a setting. In the District of

Columbia, where Foundry Church is located, the law is pretty clear:

> A priest, clergyman, rabbi, or other duly licensed, ordained, or consecrated minister of . . . religion may not be examined in any civil or criminal proceedings in the federal courts in the District of Columbia and District of Columbia courts with respect to any—(1) confession, or communication, made to him, in his professional capacity in the course of discipline enjoined by the church or other religious body to which he belongs, without the consent of the person making the confession or communication; or (2) communication made to him, in his professional capacity in the course of giving religious or spiritual advice, without the consent of the person seeking the advice. . . .

That is wise law. I am resolved to uphold the intent of that by keeping faith with such confidences. *Nothing in this book will violate pastoral confidences!*

One might ask, should a pastor ever respond to media requests and participate in the public debate—or write a book like this? What is a pastor's role or responsibility then?

The answer is that that, too, can be a part of pastoral responsibility. We are responsible for maintaining the privacy of our counseling relationships. But we are also concerned about what happens to the people we know and love. To put it in biblical language, part of our task is to care for the sheep—and part of it is to keep the wolves at bay! Thus, a pastor can want to help poor people directly, but it is also important for him or her to be an advocate for social policies that help to wipe out poverty. We want to provide a helping hand to those who have been stigmatized in society, so they will find a compassionate home in church or synagogue or mosque. But we also want to help do away with racism and other "isms" that hurt people on a wider scale. A good pastor cannot duck that responsibility, painful though it may be.

In my own case, there was yet another dimension. My academic training included a major specialization in social ethics. For more than forty years I have studied, taught, and written about the relationships between faith and the great issues of the day. That has always been an important part of my ministry. I have explored as carefully as I could the moral implications of racial discrimination, issues of war and peace, questions of economic policy, the problems and dilemmas of politics and public policy, issues of sexuality and healthy family life. I cannot claim to be an expert on all these matters, of course. But an important part of my life and vocation has been to see the connecting points between basic moral values on the one hand and the pressing issues on the other. The fact that I am not an expert on all of these things helps me to see that nobody else is either!

And so, I have felt a responsibility to participate in the significant public debates of our time, if I felt I had something to add. That has never been more true than in the present crisis affecting the president and the nation. My participation in this is not as personal counselor to people involved in it, but as one with a contribution to make. I have been confident that mine is not the only voice to be heard, indeed that it is only a minor voice. But when asked to step to the table and participate, I could not step aside. Pastors, as well as other commentators, must help discern the deeper meaning of momentous issues and the wisest courses of action in dealing with them.

While most of what I have to say or write is about moral values and the perspectives of a religious faith, there is some practical and political commentary in this book as well. I make no apology for that. I have also been a lifelong student of political thought, and I have interacted with political leaders and policymakers in the nation's capital for many years—even well before serving as pastor of a church with many such people in its congregation. In my book *Christian Perspectives on Politics*, written a decade ago, I remarked that the intersection between faith and politics is endlessly fascinating. Both are central to the human drama. I am especially interested in the ways in which one affects the other. While the present book is centered on a particular (and very important) crisis in the life of the nation, I hope my observations here will contribute to the ongoing discussions of faith and politics in our society. Nevertheless, while I wish to speak out in this way, I know that many other people have things to say that I need to hear. Those who speak out must also be prepared to listen.

THE BLUR OF THE DAYS AHEAD

Looking back on the two or three weeks following our return from the mountains, everything seems a bit blurred. The call from the media for commentators and opinion was never-ending. I accepted most of the invitations at face value and tried not to take myself too seriously in the process. That part was easier since there were so many people doing the same thing. It even helped to have letters from critics pointing out how wrong and foolish my words were. I found myself thinking, ruefully, of Jesus' words, "Woe to you when all speak well of you"(Luke 6:26). At least I had escaped that "woe"! Still, I rarely felt burned in the process. One exception involved a New England radio station. The producer had called the night before, asking if I could participate the next morning. It sounded all right, so I said yes. They called me at the appropriate time and put me on hold while the talk show host finished his introduction. Listening to that, I could scarcely believe the hate and filth that poured forth. I hung up. When the producer called me back to say that we had been disconnected, I could only say, "I'm sorry, but I will not participate in that gutter conversation." That was the exception, as I said, but it served to remind me of the dark side of the national debate, where sacred values are besmirched even by those who purport to defend them. On the whole, I was glad we had come down from the woods. There were things to be said.

The president was in my prayers during the time of his testimony to the grand jury on August 17. I had no idea what he would be saying, although I knew it would be a grueling experience for him as it would be for anyone. Through the day there were media rumors that he would make a statement to the nation sometime in the evening. The announcement came after 6:00 that he had completed his testimony. There were the usual "leaks" about what had been said, some of which proved to be true, some utterly unfounded, and there was an announcement that he would indeed speak to the nation later in the evening.

Along with sixty or seventy million fellow Americans, I heard him speak. "I did have a relationship with Miss Lewinsky that was not appropriate. In fact, it was wrong. It constituted a critical lapse in judgment and a personal failure on my part for which I am solely and completely responsible." He acknowledged that he had misled people and said, "I deeply regret that." He voiced his determination to do "whatever it takes" to put it right. Additionally, he criticized the independent counsel investigation.

I was a bit surprised by the brevity of the president's statement. Even more, I was disappointed by his confirmation that he had indeed engaged in serious misconduct. I had hoped otherwise. In the months since the story first broke in January, I had said that I viewed the charges and allegations with skepticism. That was not quite the same as saying that I was sure they were false, for I could not be certain of that. But the way in which they had come forth, combined with the number of stories that could not be confirmed reliably, really did lead me to be doubtful about the charges. There might have been something there, but nothing approaching the allegations. So the president's statement to the nation came as unpleasant confirmation that he really had done things that were very wrong.

My initial reaction to the brief speech was that he had probably said what he needed to say. To this day I cannot understand the critics who took the president to task for not saying he was sorry or for not apologizing. Perhaps he should have said more. Perhaps he should have spoken more directly to the hurt of people directedly affected and the grief this had caused the nation. Perhaps he should have spoken then of what he intended to do to set things right. Much of this he did say in the weeks to come. But when the president declared that his conduct had been "wrong," I thought that was the clear and unambiguous word to use. If you say you're "sorry," that can just mean you're sorry you got caught. He wasn't saying he was sorry he got caught; he was saying that what he got caught doing had been wrong. In retrospect it may have been a mistake for him to aim an oblique criticism at the independent counsel's operation. I will say more about that later in this book, but such criticism might, with greater grace, have been left to others. At the time I could imagine he was stirred up by the afternoon encounter. Maybe this would have been a good time to count to ten or even to save his speech for the next day. Still, I thought his brief address was pretty forthright.

That, of course, was not the assessment of numbers of commentators that night and in the days to come. A number of people, beginning with former vice president Dan Quayle, even called for his resignation. Many of those who didn't go that far still demanded more of a statement, more of an apology, a clearer indication that he was genuinely sorry. The following day, August 18, the president and his family headed to Martha's Vineyard for their own time of vacation and healing. During that period he made a couple of public appearances during which he amplified the statement of repentance. He voiced that repeatedly in private as well and welcomed statements by friends confirming and underscoring his repentance. I was among those who were in a position to make such statements, because he had spoken directly to me about his remorse over his conduct, in such a way that I had to take it seriously. I reported this publicly when assured by the president that he welcomed such a reinforcement of his own public statements. Thus, I did not feel that this would violate any pastoral confidences. When asked in a public meeting whether I was being "used" by the president, I replied that I did not think so. But if I was being "used" I was happy to be used to underscore a public apology which he had needed to make. I had no reason to doubt his sincerity.

But repentance is not easy. It may, in fact, be more a process than a single act. We become more aware of what we have really done, the full meaning of our actions becomes clearer to us, we realize the hurt we have inflicted on others. A public figure who is put in the position of having to repeat something over and over again in order to satisfy critics, some of whom doubtless would not have been content with any combination of words, faces especially tough going. Nevertheless, the president understood that his capacity to lead depended very much on his words of repentance being sincere and being taken seriously.

In the midst of all this, at the conclusion of the vacation time, he and Mrs. Clinton went to Russia for a long-anticipated summit conference with President Boris Yeltsin. The press at that conference seemed concerned only with the scandal back home, even though the issues facing Russia and the relationship between the United States and Russia were very important. From Russia the Clintons traveled to Northern Ireland. There they were greeted by large and enthusiastic crowds that hailed the president for his central role in the negotiation of peace between Protestants and Catholics.

Returning to Washington, the president faced a continuing drumbeat of criticism, centering on the adequacy of his confession and apology and his continuing fitness to serve. Speculation began to center on when the special prosecutor's report would be delivered to Congress and what it would contain. The Report was somewhat ceremoniously delivered to Congress on September 9 in the form of 445 pages and sixteen large boxes of supporting documents and tapes. The Report was understood to lay out the case for impeachment of the president. After brief deliberation, the U.S. House of Representatives voted that the Report should be released to the public. It was announced that this would be done on Friday, September 11. The stage was set.

— 2 —

The Prayer Breakfast and the Starr Report

I woke up early on Friday, September 11. I had agreed to appear on a couple of early morning network programs. The interviews were in anticipation of a prayer breakfast to be held later in the morning at the White House, which I had been invited to attend. On one of the programs, I found myself paired with the Reverend Paige Patterson, president of the Southern Baptist Convention, who had been calling for President Clinton's resignation and who repeated that call on the program. I sought to place the prayer breakfast in context and to underscore the importance of both repentance and forgiveness. I do not recall my exact words, but I emphasized that if the essence of morality is love, the nation's hurt cannot be healed in a loveless spirit. I disagreed with Reverend Patterson about resignation. It would be a tragic thing for the country for its president to be forced from office over this matter, I said.

I hastened to the White House for the prayer breakfast.

Even though I had spoken about the prayer breakfast on this and another program, I truly did not know quite what to expect. I was even a bit fearful. Undoubtedly the issue of the day would come up; surely the president himself would bring it up in his opening remarks. The usual format at these events calls for an initial presidential statement in the presence of the press and television, after which the media is excused and the assembled religious leaders are given an opportunity to voice their questions or concerns. I worried about what those might be. There were some 125 guests. They represented a very wide spectrum of American religious life. I knew many of them personally, but not most of them. A few religious leaders had recently called for the president's resignation. I could picture, with dread, a scene in which several would do that in his presence and then repeat it in front of waiting cameras outside. I was seated next to a White House staffer at a table for eight or ten. She greeted everybody cordially, although I think she was also a little nervous about the direction the gathering might take. The group at our table was diverse, ethnically and religiously.

The program began with a prayer that captured the deep feelings of the moment. Vice President Gore then spoke of his support for the president before introducing him. President Clinton stood to speak. He said he had struggled with what he was to say far into the night, and his tired face confirmed that. Reading from his hand-written notes he voiced his deep feelings of remorse over his misbehavior, including his regret over the pain he had caused his own family, the Lewinsky family, others directly involved, and the nation. He offered no excuses. He blamed no one but himself. Regarding the Starr investigation, he acknowledged that for himself it might even have been a blessing because it had made him face up to his need to change. It was not, in any case, a time for anger. He noted that he would be working on changing his life, relying especially on pastoral help. He was determined that his behavior not be repeated. He spoke of his need for forgiveness, from God and from those whom he had hurt. It was an emotional statement. Such a message might have been more helpful the night of his testimony than his brief address to the nation had been. In reflecting on this, I reminded myself again that repentance is a process. These weeks had been necessary for him to see the larger picture of his own life and responsibility.

We had breakfast then, expecting to take up comments or questions later. But during breakfast one after another of those present approached the president personally to express their spiritual support for him. Soon an impromptu line formed—and another to greet the First Lady in the same way. Almost everybody participated. The president was to speak at a memorial service at the National Cathedral later in the morning, so there did not turn out to be much time for questions or comments. But neither was there much need. All of the comments made directly to the president and Mrs. Clinton were warm, supportive, forgiving. It surprised me that virtually everybody present felt that way.

Some who were not there may have wondered if forgiveness was offered in the spirit of what theologian

Dietrich Bonhoeffer called "cheap grace"—that is, for-giveness without real repentance and change on the part of the one being forgiven. Perhaps that was the spirit of some present; I do not know. But I do not believe that was the attitude of most. Rather, I believe forgiveness was offered out of respect for serious repentance by somebody who really had been humbled. These religious leaders of many faiths understood that we all stand in need of forgiveness. This was, I thought, a deeply religious moment, and it was enhanced, not diminished, by the great diversity of religious faiths represented there. It seemed to me that the attitudes of the prayer breakfast participants were an expression of the nation at its best, not its ugliest or its meanest, which we had seen so often in recent years. Quite apart from the present crisis, it struck me afresh that so diverse a country could find in its vastly different religious traditions a deeper basis of unity. That is a hopeful sign for the nation and for the world.

The president's statement had been broadcast live on several of the networks. It was repeated or excerpted on television through the day and printed in a number of leading newspapers the following day. I was interviewed by several newspapers and on several television programs through the day by reporters who wanted my views on the breakfast and what it might mean. I emphasized the importance of forgiveness, redemption, and restoration in the midst of a grave national crisis. I asked, could the nation respond on that level?

That afternoon a very different focus developed. The Starr Report was released through the internet. Most of the networks interrupted their regular programming to download the Report, barely edited, with the raw details of sexual encounters included. It was as though the networks were vying among themselves to be first to get it out. Then the commentators took over, explaining what it all meant. The spirit of this part of the day was demonstrated in a search for incriminating details. Only late that night, after concluding a last interview, could I pause to review this incredible day. It was as though there were two tracks at work: the one emphasizing the moral acts of repentance and forgiveness and the spiritual unity of the nation, the other focusing on judgment and condemnation. Which of these really represents our country? It was as if the country was struggling to define its own soul.

A SERMON TAKES SHAPE

The next day was Saturday. I had been working on my Sunday sermon for some days, but it had not quite jelled. I was tired, and yet I knew this could be one of the most important moments of spiritual and moral leadership in my whole preaching ministry. There was a real possibility that the Clintons would be present. Whenever they are, so are many representatives of the White House press corps. The audience is therefore potentially much larger than the gathered congregation. I had preached to the first family many times over the past few years. They had become a part of the regular worshiping congregation at Foundry, their privacy respected and no particular notice taken. But now we were in the middle of an indescribably important national crisis, one in which moral and spiritual values were central. I did not and do not want to take my role too seriously. And yet, how often does a preacher have to carry such a burden? In the five and a half years they have attended our church, the Clintons have never tried to determine the contents of a Sunday sermon. I felt no pressure on that score. Nonetheless, on this occasion I wanted to draw as deeply as possibly on the love which is at the heart of our faith.

The setting for the sermon was fairly commonplace. That particular Sunday was to be Foundry's start-of-the-school-year emphasis on the church's education program, with the dedication of teachers to their task and a sermon emphasizing the importance of education and spiritual growth. The sermon title, "A Call to Christian Maturity," had been set months earlier. Now I had the task of including, somehow, the great issue of the day. The title was apt enough! Everybody's maturity was being put to the test. But how should the sermon be developed? That was not yet clear—and Sunday morning was getting dangerously close.

That Saturday evening, with much work still to do, I honored a commitment to appear on one of the nationally broadcast TV talk shows. I was sorry I had agreed to that; I really needed the time to polish the sermon. There were delays at the studio that cost more time. When the program began I discovered that the two other religious participants were very condemnatory of the president and that the moderator was as well. I agreed with them that the president's misbehavior could not be condoned, though I disagreed with their sweeping condemnations of his character. The discussion came to a head when I was asked point-blank by the moderator about my own judgment of the president's character. I made clear that I could not condone his behavior in this matter, but I also said none of us was in a position to condemn him as a person.

After leaving the studio I continued work on the sermon. Finally it began to come together. I would even use one interchange from the TV program to help illustrate what I was to say, so the interview time was not really wasted. I would begin the sermon by dealing with the education theme, as I had intended, by emphasizing two things: first, the positive value we place on the mind, encouraging free inquiry and thoughtful faith, and second, the importance of love as the basis of all moral and spiritual growth. The second point would lead directly into the big issue of the day. It would be a sermon for the church, of course, but it would also be for the nation. It went something like this:

A SERMON FOR THE CHURCH AND THE NATION

Once again we gather at a time of great consequence. We pause before the largeness of the issues. We wonder if any of us can ever be adequate to deal with them. In a sense that's unusual; in a sense it's not. For every time we gather, we humbly worship the One who is vastly greater than ourselves. We trust that God will use whatever is helpful and, in the spirit of an old Middle Eastern proverb, "with the breath of kindness, blow the rest away."

I committed myself to the sermon title many months ago, but as this week has progressed it has seemed more and more timely. What could be more helpful, now, than conversation about spiritual maturity? Our focus is specifically on the church's education program, and the title is clearly appropriate for that. Christian education is *about* Christian maturity. In a sense, that is what the church is about in every aspect of its life. The scripture texts were also selected months ago, including the passage in Proverbs and the two passages from Paul's great First Letter to the Corinthians, which both deal with spiritual maturity.

Paul's letter was addressed to what we could call "new Christians." These are people who do not become Christians through birth and nurture but by conversion at a later point in life, people who often feel great joy in finding and experiencing the love of God for the first time. Paul speaks to them about their transports of joy, which they expressed through speaking in tongues, that is, verbalization without recognizable words but with deep feeling. This kind of spiritual outpouring was very real in the life of the early church, including the church in Corinth. And notice what Paul says about that:

> I thank God that I speak in tongues more than all of you; nevertheless, in church I would rather speak five words with my mind, in order to instruct others also, than ten thousand words in a tongue. Brothers and sisters, do not be children in your thinking; rather, be infants in evil, but in thinking be adults. (14:18–20)

Now, what are we to make of that? I do not think that Paul is calling for a purely intellectual approach to the faith. Christian faith is not simply a matter of mental correctness; it is not just a "head trip." Earlier in First Corinthians, in the second chapter (vv. 1–5), Paul had also written these words:

When I came to you, brothers and sisters, I did not come proclaiming the mystery of God to you in lofty words or wisdom. For I decided to know nothing among you except Jesus Christ, and him crucified. And I came to you in weakness and in fear, and much trembling. My speech and my proclamation were not with plausible words of wisdom, but with a demonstration of the Spirit and of power, so that your faith might rest not on human wisdom but on the power of God.

Well, Paul is speaking of the fundamental foundation of the faith: "Jesus Christ, and him crucified."

With Paul this is not just an abstract formula to be acknowledged so we can be saved. It means Jesus on a real cross, with all its shame, bitterness, suffering. What Paul is saying is that Jesus Christ on the cross is the supreme expression of the love of God. And if we don't start with the love of God, we don't start at all. That's the foundation. Everything else is growth on that foundation. If that foundation isn't there, no growth is possible. Of course, that has vast implications for Christian education. To teach love is not just to speak of it—it is to *be* love. My hope for the children of this and every church is that as they grow up love *defines* the church for them—so that when they become adults they will look back upon their church experience as being defined in that way. Maybe they will have to unlearn some things later, but they will never have to unlearn that. It will remain the foundation for all of their later growth.

The importance of learning love through actual experience is conveyed beautifully in a poem by Dorothy Law Nolte. This is a part of what she had to say:

If children live with criticism, they learn to condemn.
If children live with hostility, they learn to fight.
If children live with fear, they learn to be apprehensive.
If children live with pity, they learn to feel sorry
    for themselves.

If children live with ridicule, they learn to feel shy.
If children live with shame, they learn to feel guilty.

But then she adds,

If children live with encouragement, they learn confidence.
If children live with tolerance, they learn patience.
If children live with praise, they learn appreciation.
If children live with acceptance, they learn to love.
If children live with approval, they learn to like themselves.

Such simple points are spelled out in greater detail in Ms. Nolte's new book, *Children Learn What They Live*. But that's the fundamental, to live the life of love.

Intellectual growth also matters. What does Paul mean when he writes, "I would rather speak five words with my mind than ten thousand words in a tongue"? The ten thousand words are an expression of feeling. Feeling, particularly the feeling of love, is basic to all moral and spiritual growth. But it is also important that we use our minds as we grow in the faith. I can think of numbers of ways in which the life of the intellect is important to us. You know, even at the most rudimentary level, how important it is to learn to read. Without being able to read, we cannot even read the Bible! It was a great breakthrough for Western Christianity when the Bible was translated into the vernacular and printed on the first printing presses, and people were able to read the Bible! That helped in the spiritual journey. Today we have many additional writings to help us along the way, but our use of such resources depends largely upon that intellectual skill.

How important it also is to be able to question, and not to feel guilty about our doubts and uncertainties. I've known people who felt that there were some doctrines of faith that were so far above criticism, that if you had any doubts, you needed to suppress them. But we can't suppress doubts successfully. They'll still be there. There's only one way to deal with them: We have to work them through, and an important part of that is *thinking* them through. Sometimes we find ourselves at peace, having gone above our doubts. Sometimes we have learned to grow beyond old views into new insights. But if we're afraid to think, our growth can stop right there. I was on a program some years ago with a political leader from another country, who said with great sadness that he had had to leave his church because he could no longer accept one of its doctrines honestly. The doctrine in question was fairly minor. What a tragedy, I thought, that he was not encouraged by his church to use his mind. He couldn't stay in the church and grow, and the church was deprived of his gifted mind and honest spirit.

And, of course, intellectual growth also means moving beyond conventional wisdom and popular prejudices of all kinds. How many illustrations we've had throughout the history of the church, of conventional wisdom and prejudice that really demeaned people, made it hard for people to grow and participate in the life of the community. How long it took for Christian churches of this land to understand, first, that slavery was wrong and, then, that racism was wrong. How long it has taken the church in general to see that women are fully as capable as men of thinking and providing leadership. James Russell Lowell's hymn poem includes the line "time makes ancient good uncouth." Time also helps us see the wisdom of much ancient good. But Lowell was certainly right about the baggage of old ignorance and prejudice. A fair amount of damage has been done by kindly disposed people who were just wrong, because they hadn't thought enough or studied enough about particular issues or were still captive to inherited cultural prejudices. We need to study together, to think together. I think Paul had many such objectives in mind: to build up, to grow together, to work toward the common goal of Christian maturity.

Today we face momentous issues in the life of our nation. What does the call to Christian maturity mean to us? Do the churches have an important message to bring to our land, to ourselves, to our people in this moment of crisis? I have thought long thoughts about that these recent weeks, especially in this past week. It all seemed to come to focus last Friday. It was as if there were two paths along which American culture is moving, two very different ways of understanding where we are as a people.

The first path was the Prayer Breakfast which occurred at the White House on Friday. I had the privilege of being a part of that, and to experience that directly. I felt that I was representing all of you there. In that setting there were maybe a hundred and twenty or thirty religious leaders, representing many different kinds of American faiths: Protestant, Catholic, Jewish, Muslim, Hindu, Sikh. The president spoke words that probably most of you have seen or heard, because it was televised and replayed a good deal through the day. His were words of deep repentance and contrition. I feel that I know this man well enough to know that the message really came from his heart. He did not seek to excuse his conduct in any way. He even said that others might criticize the process, but for him maybe it was a blessing. Because it forced him to face up to things that he'd long needed to face up to. And he committed himself to the hard work of repentance, knowing that repentance is not just the work of the moment. Sometimes it's the work of a lifetime—coming to terms with what brought you to where you are, why you're there, and where the road is ahead to get you away from there and to be able to grow. And in that context with these religious leaders, with no exception that I could see in the room, he was enveloped in a climate of forgiveness and caring. These representatives of religious groups from across the land were concerned to be a part of his healing and to go forth from that place to speak about it. That was path one on Friday.

The second path was the Starr Report as it came out in lurid detail, breathlessly portrayed on television screens all over the country, without too much of an effort to edit it, enveloped in a climate of judgment replete with questions about punishment.

I found myself wondering, as the day wore on, which of these events defines the *soul* of America? Which represents who we really are as a people? One does not want to oversimplify, and yet there is a watershed here of immense importance: the way of repentance and forgiveness or the way of judgment and punishment.

I found myself thinking back again to the story of the woman caught in sin. I wondered what it might have been if they'd really done it, if they'd stoned her to death. The law called for it. Jesus was being tested about the law. He stopped them. But what if they had stoned her to death? What would the effect of that have been on the moral life and development of the people of that village? Would they have grown morally? It's a little like the old scapegoating system, where the sins of the community are laid on the back of a goat and the goat is driven from the community, and that's how you deal with the sin. I think the message might rather have been, "Don't get caught. Avoid getting in trouble." But there would have been no moral growth. And I thought of Jesus in that role. He had to hold the sharks at bay, in order then to be able to say to her, "Go, and sin no more."

That was that situation. Where are we as a people? It would be a lot easier to deal with this if we could single out somebody and say, well, here's the sinner-in-chief. But we cannot do that. I was on another of those talk shows last night that have been dealing with the crisis. There was a fair amount of self-righteousness floating in the air, if I can say this in a non-judgmental way. In response, I said something like this: "You know, these sins that we've been hearing about all day—I've been married for forty-two years, and I love my wife very much, and I haven't done any of that! But I have to tell you that if the president of the United States were here, I could not stand in front of him and say, 'Bill Clinton, I'm a better man than you are.' I could not say that. And you folks, the ones who are also on this program, you can't say that either."

We're dealing with a very widespread problem here. The root of the problem, in very large measure, is that our culture is one in which sex has gotten separated from love and commitment. The signals of that are everywhere. I agree with people who feel pornography is a corrupting influence in our society. But some of those very people seemed so anxious to put pornography—as included in the Starr Report—in the newspapers this week! The point is not that sex is bad—sex itself is good. But sex separated from love and commitment can lead to evil. It can be destructive. The national crisis provides a case study of that, for all to see. But there are many other illustrations of that, buried away in all the nooks and crannies of our national life.

How are we going to deal with that? Are we going to take one person and heap the sins of the nation on him, and feel free of those sins ourselves? Or, are we going to do the harder work of corporate repentance that draws all of us in, and helps us all to grow in love? Without the prospect of forgiveness and love, there can be no real repentance or change. The very essence of all morality is love. We cannot deal with evils in society on a foundation other than love. That is the prophetic word we all need to hear. The greatest of the prophets in the biblical tradition were people who did not point at somebody else and say, "There is the sinner." The greatest were the ones who went to God and said, "O God, have mercy on *us*, a nation of sinners." That is the more prophetic word.

My friends, this has been a trying time. How often in these days have I been grateful for you, in this beloved congregation, your understanding and support. I have been able to feel that, even though you might disagree with this or that that I might say, still you were holding me in your prayers. When called upon to speak to much wider media audiences, I have felt your prayers that the words spoken might help in the healing of the nation. I have often found myself thinking of those words of Paul: "Now we see in a glass darkly . . . but then face to face." How we all have yearned to see it all face to face, here and now! The ultimate truths about what is at stake in situations like this, and the greatest wisdom to guide us, often seem obscure. "We see in a glass darkly." What are we to say, then, about life as we must actually live it? What are we to say in the brokenness of our humanity as we await the time when we shall see it all face to face? "Now abide these three, faith, hope, and love. *And the greatest of these is love."*

Concluding with those words from the thirteenth chapter of First Corinthians, I asked the congregation to join in singing John Greenleaf Whittier's hymn of repentance:

Dear Lord and Father of mankind, forgive our
    foolish ways,
Reclothe us in our rightful mind, in purer lives thy
    service find,
In deeper reverence, praise.

That, in essence, was the sermon delivered that Sunday, September 13. I had thought the president would be there. All of the Secret Service arrangements were in place, and it seemed likely. I had guessed right about the congregation. They were interested in the Christian education theme, but that morning they obviously wanted the pulpit to deal with the crisis at hand.

Toward the end of the first service (we have two on Sunday mornings), I was handed a note. The president had asked me to call him at the White House as soon as possible. I hastened to my office and soon was deep in conversation with him. It was not going to be possible for the Clintons to attend church, but still we spoke together about the theme of the morning. I related the essential points of the sermon, and we talked about it. The next day's newspapers reported that the president had "skipped church." They didn't know, however, that he had nonetheless heard the sermon and that he had been deeply engaged in the message of the morning service.

ANOTHER SUNDAY, ANOTHER SERMON

The following Sunday presented a similar problem for the preacher, but with this difference: To the surprise of many, the Starr Report had not been nearly as damaging to the president as most people had predicted. Public opinion continued to affirm his continuation in office, if anything by wider margins. There wasn't quite as much crisis in the air. Still, the issue continued to be central in the consciousness of large numbers of people.

This time, the Clintons were, in fact, present. The service celebrated the church's outstanding music program, led by Dr. Eileen Guenther, and dedicated the choirs and other worship leaders. The sermon was based on Psalm

137, with its theme "How could we sing the Lord's song in a foreign land?" In abridged form, it went like this:

Psalm 137 is one of the most poignant passages in scripture. It was written by an unknown author during one of Israel's greatest crises—the exile in Babylon. Perhaps you already know the story. The Babylonian armies had descended on little Judah, captured the city of Jerusalem, destroying its walls and, most cruelly, its temple. That was especially important, because the temple was where the Lord was understood to live. So the spiritual core of the nation was crushed. Just to make sure there would be no rebellion, the Babylonians then transported the leadership class of the country into exile in Babylon. The exiles were not especially mistreated, at least not physically. But, as the Psalm suggests, they were tormented both by grief and by the "trash talk" of their captors. Would they please entertain Babylon with some good Jewish music?! This is the way Psalm 137 (vv. 1–6) describes the scene:

> By the rivers of Babylon—there we sat down and there we wept when we remembered Zion. On the willows there we hung up our harps. For there our captors asked us for songs, and our tormentors asked for mirth, saying, "Sing us one of the songs of Zion!" How could we sing the Lord's song in a foreign land? If I forget you, O Jerusalem, let my right hand wither! Let my tongue cling to the roof of my mouth, if I do not remember you, if I do not set Jerusalem above my highest joy.

How can we sing "Zion's songs" in Babylon? How indeed! The mood of the exiles was not just grief—there was also deep bitterness. In designating Psalm 137 as the Old Testament scripture, I thought to omit the sheer *hatred* of verses 8–9. But then it dawned on me that those verses provide the most graphic evidence of just how alienated the

Hebrew captives felt in Babylon. It helps us see why it was so difficult to "sing the Lord's song" in the foreign land.

> O daughter Babylon, you devastator! Happy shall they be who pay you back what you have done to us! Happy shall they be who take your little ones and dash them against the rock!

I'd like to think that the author of Psalm 137 would not ever have done such awful things. But the words do convey the depth of bitterness alongside the intense grief.

The Psalm, taken as a whole, anticipates part of the New Testament lesson from Matthew—the one in which Jesus said we should not cast our pearls before swine. That is a very interesting metaphor. Our "pearls" represent the things that are most precious to us, our basic values and traditions. When we expose them to those who are contemptuous of them, we cheapen them. So the Hebrews in exile asked, How can we sing the songs of Zion in Babylon? All that was most precious to them was embodied in those songs. Now, in exile, were they supposed to parade their spiritual treasures only to have them scorned by the Babylonians? "Do not throw your pearls before swine, or they will trample them under foot and turn and maul you." So, sing the "songs of Zion" in Babylon? Would that not cheapen them? Maybe better to endure in silence and bitterness.

In a certain sense, we are always "singing the Lord's song in a foreign land." People of faith always exist in a larger cultural context that is alien to much that their faith stands for. It is easy to see that when in a really hostile setting, such as existed in Communist countries during the Cold War or in Nazi Germany.

In our own country we do not live amidst police state conditions. Does that mean that the Psalm has nothing to say to us? Of course not. Ours is not a society that fully supports Judeo-Christian values. So we too must ask ourselves, how can we sing the Lord's song in a foreign land?

How can we sing the Lord's song in a land where there is

still so much poverty and so many of God's little ones suffer? How can we sing the Lord's song in a land where millions, young and old, suffer from the blight of drugs and alcoholism? How can we sing the Lord's song in a land where violent crime spreads terror and destruction, greatly facilitated by easy access to firearms? How can we sing the Lord's song in a land where the language of God's love is equated with weakness, and the language of self-righteousness is equated with morality? How can we sing the Lord's song in a land where, on a truly vast scale, God's gift of sex is separated from loving commitment? How can we sing the Lord's song in a land where public discourse is so clouded by partisan bitterness?

I am especially concerned about that as we gather here today. The democratic institutions of our society have endured, intact, for more than two centuries. They depend upon a willingness by those who struggle for power to observe some restraints. Above all, there must be a willingness to accept, and even welcome, a responsible opposition. But far too many politicians in our time seem eager, not just to defeat but to destroy their opponents. Both parties are increasingly prone to fight their political battles in that spirit. But when public leaders seek to destroy their opponents they will wind up destroying the nation!

Not all who live in this land are like that. I believe most are not. Yet these are realities that muffle the Lord's song or hold the Lord's song in derision. How *are* we to "sing the Lord's song," when so much of life here—and everywhere—seems so far removed from its melodies and harmonies?

Music can, in fact, play the wrong kind of role. It can be used in such a way that our sensitivities to human suffering and injustice are not awakened but deadened. Do you remember the scornful words of the prophet Amos?

Alas for those who lie on beds of ivory, and lounge on their couches, and eat lambs from the flock, and calves from the stall; who sing idle songs to the sound of the harp, and like David improvise on instruments of music; who drink wine from bowls, and anoint themselves with the finest oils, but are not grieved over the ruin of [the land of] Joseph!" (Amos 6:4–6)

He also is the one who spoke what he considered to be the word of the Lord:

I hate, I despise your festivals, and I take no delight in your solemn assemblies. . . . Take away from me the noise of your songs; I will not listen to the melody of your harps. But let justice roll down like waters, and righteousness like an ever-flowing stream. (Amos 5:21, 23–24)

Well, Amos is right. Music and worship *can* obscure the realities of suffering and injustice in a broken world. Amos is right. When music plays that role it diminishes our humanity, it does not enhance it. But that is not the whole story. Music can make us *more* sensitive; it can energize us for the great moral struggles of our time. Music can draw us closer to the greatness and beauty of God. Great music has its source in God; it expresses the rhythms and melodies and harmonies of an inexhaustible universe and the great heart of its Creator. It can thus reinforce our commitment to God; it can help us see that our true humanity can find its home only in God. We are made to feel, perhaps in new ways, our closeness to a large body of fellow Christians—and to the much larger body of people worldwide who are not Christian but who are just as beloved of God as if they were. We are sensitized anew to human values that are often obscured by the worst elements in our culture.

Those who experienced the Civil Rights movement most directly could not help noticing the role music played there. The Civil Rights songs—like "We Shall Overcome" and "We Shall Not Be Moved"—had their origins in gospel hymns. It was interesting to see, in the midst of the most intense conflict, how the freedom songs emerged, on the spot, line by line, as very ordinary people gave voice to their deepest convictions and commitments. *I cannot imagine Amos deriding that!* This was music in harmony with the cascading waters of justice and righteousness.

Foundry is blessed by extraordinary music. It reflects the diversities of many musical traditions, all expressed with great artistic grace. It would be easy in a church such as ours for the music to be a soothing distraction. But that is not so among us! The music of this church is a part of what sends us forth into a broken world to do the Lord's work. As we have commissioned our music and worship leaders anew today, so have we also commissioned them and us for that work in the world.

How shall we sing the Lord's song in a foreign land? *Joyously*, for God lives, even in Babylon, and the language of God is love, even in Babylon. How shall we sing the Lord's song? *Hopefully*, for we know that God's loving will is going to prevail. How shall we sing the Lord's song? *Faithfully*, for we know that God will take all of our small efforts and turn them into good on a scale we cannot imagine.

THE ISSUE IS JOINED

After completing these two sermons, the most important issue posed by the presidential crisis had become increasingly clear to me: Will we be a society that is grounded in compassion and a generous spirit—as exemplified by the themes of the White House prayer breakfast and the response by the religious leaders? Or will we allow ourselves to be increasingly hard-hearted, as exemplified by the Starr Report and the manner of its presentation to the nation?

I do not suppose for a moment that any great nation could ever be solely the one or the other. A generous spirit is not altogether lacking among those who follow the special prosecutor's lead and among those in the media who have so sensationalized it all. Nor are those who want to follow the path of forgiveness altogether saintly or even necessarily consistent in practice. But the issue is which spirit will dominate the culture and which will be expressed in our society's actual decision-making.

Have I oversimplified here? Perhaps we need to examine more closely some of the key questions that have been raised in the national debate. I have struggled with these questions. I wish I could say I have them all neatly settled. I do not. But now is certainly the time to discuss them.

— 3 —

Hard Questions about Love, Sex, and Social Controls

The crisis has been about a lot more than sex, but perhaps we should begin there. What is there about sexual behavior and misbehavior that excites such interest? Why are we so much like the *Wall Street Journal* columnist Al Hunt, who wrote concerning the Starr Report, "It is sleazy. It is kinky. It is repulsive and I couldn't wait to turn the page"? Why is it that some of the most puritanical people in our society seem so fascinated by pornography, so eager to expose its immoral effects on our culture, *in such detail?* Why is it that those who seem most "liberated" in their attitudes toward sex turn strangely prudish and moralistic when scandal breaks?

Some, at least according to the polls, have considered the whole question of sexual behavior to be a nonissue. For them it is as though sex has nothing to do with morality. I cannot accept that, nor do most thoughtful people. Sex, on one level, is a wonderful gift from God. It is not only for procreation but for an expression of intimate love. It can be humanizing in the best sense of the word. Sex, on another level, can be an arena for self-centeredness and crude exploitation, even violence. It can be dehumanizing.

The church has often had a hard time dealing with this. One of the greatest of Christian thinkers, Augustine, exemplified the problem. By his own admission, Augustine was sexually irresponsible in his early adult years. Upon his conversion, he believed that sexual activity was at the heart of his troubled spiritual life; sex had become his god. In his later reflections, Augustine spoke of spiritual fulfillment in the love of God. That fulfillment comes, he wrote, when we love God even to the point of being contemptuous of ourselves. By contrast, we are only creatures of this earth when we love ourselves to the point of contempt for God. Self-love, ironically, destroys the self. Only through the love of God do we find ourselves. As Augustine put it in a beautiful little prayer, "Thou hast made us for thyself, and our hearts are restless until they find their rest in thee." We find our true humanity in the love of God, and the love of God draws us ever more deeply into the love of one another.

Augustine died in 430 A.D., but his writings put a decisive stamp on Christian culture for a thousand years. His emphasis upon the love of God was the central theological theme throughout the Middle Ages. Even today, his ideas remain very important among Christian theologians.

Augustine's own sexual history, however, may also have contributed a discordant note to our culture today. He may have made it more difficult for subsequent generations to see the intrinsic goodness of sex when it is expressed in loving commitment, simply because it had not been expressed in that way in his early life. Without ever experiencing such commitment and upon his conversion, he became celibate. Neither he nor later Christian thinkers regarded sex in marriage as "wrong." Still, with many such thinkers there remained something a bit questionable about sex. Celibacy could be seen as a higher calling.

I wonder if that theological legacy does not continue to haunt our culture. The very fact that we are so fascinated by sexual scandal may be revealing. Why is it that even so many of those who are bitterly opposed to pornography seem to want to talk about it so much, to expose it in such detail? Are they themselves, at some unconscious level, under the power of sex as a form of idolatry? I do not say this in judgment of those who oppose pornography. I join them in that, for I believe it is truly a corrupting influence in society.

And yet here is the issue: If the root problem with pornography or sexual misbehavior is the disconnection between the gift of sex and loving commitment—so that sex has become a form of self-centeredness or selfish exploitation of others—then how are individuals and societies to grow out of that? Can they do it by exposing and condemning the excesses, meanwhile titillating the onlookers? How can it be done without somehow rediscovering *love?* And how can love be rediscovered in an unloving way?

Let's be clear about this. It is possible for behavior, that

of individuals and of whole societies, to be controlled by
sheer determination, willpower, law, and custom. Every
society, in fact, needs a fabric of such controls. As
individuals, we need stabilizing habits and external checks
to keep us steady. But do these checks and habits make us
more *moral* as individuals? Do they make a community or
a whole society more *moral?* Not if the essence of morality
is love! Somehow these external factors must find their
place in the service of love. Otherwise, they can even get
in the way of love. That may not seem so, but the self-
righteousness that often develops around our sense of
moral accomplishment is the very antithesis of love. Jesus
had a lot to say about morality, but he reserved his most
scathing rebukes, not for people who have fallen into sin
through weakness (and who need to mature and grow
spiritually) but for those who are self-righteous and
hypocritical. Those are the ones who need to become
more humble.

It is tempting for a community to deal with problems
of immorality by publicly condemning the most visible
sinners. In the present situation, I have been impressed
by how widely the sin is shared! The disconnection
between sex and loving commitment is pervasive in our
culture. We are bombarded with it. Even the very
newspapers that editorially have condemned the
president in scathing language are vehicles in all sorts of
ways for the disconnection, in the news they carry, in
the pictures they show, in the gossip they repeat. The
late night TV shows, loaded these months with ridicule
of the president and ribald humor, are purveyors of

exactly that crude treatment of sex. All of this sends a very mixed message.

THE NECESSITY AND DIFFICULTY OF FORGIVENESS

The debate, as it has developed in America, has featured the question of forgiveness. Many, like those who attended the prayer breakfast, wish to forgive the president and move on. Others will allow for forgiveness, provided we can be sure the repentance is sufficiently sincere and the consequences of the behavior are not avoided. Still others feel that the behavior is unforgivable. The latter group includes a handful who have written some of the most hateful letters I have ever received—but I do not think they represent a majority even of this group.

I was attracted to a comment attributed to the Reverend Rex Horne, the pastor of President Clinton's home church in Little Rock, Arkansas. Reverend Horne said that the president's conduct in the Lewinsky matter was "indefensible, but not unforgiveable." Even some of the president's severest critics would have agreed with that. On one television program I found myself in the company of the Reverend Jerry Falwell. The conservative preacher had been calling for the president's resignation—and repeated the call on that program. Still, even Falwell spoke the language of forgiveness. God forgives, he said, and so should we. But, Reverend Falwell continued, the president's actions had disqualified him for his high post, just as a clergyman who sins in this way should leave his position and seek healing in a more private setting. It is difficult for me to see how a Christian could fail to go at least as far as Reverend Falwell has in forgiving others, and many Christians would not attach the penalty of removal from office to their forgiveness.

To a Christian, all forgiveness is based on God's forgiveness. As Paul puts it, "All have sinned and fall short of the glory of God." Therefore, he asks, "What becomes of boasting?" "It is excluded." We all depend upon God's grace, originally a Roman legal term referring to the pardon given by the magistrate in a legal proceeding. We have all sinned, but God is gracious, God forgives. Otherwise, we would all be in peril. It is therefore incumbent upon all of us to forgive. The Lord's Prayer includes the line "Forgive us our sins as we forgive those who sin against us," which makes a direct connection between our own need for forgiveness and our willingness to forgive others. In the version of the Lord's Prayer contained in the Gospel of Matthew, the line about forgiveness is singled out as central to the prayer's meaning: "For if you forgive others their trespasses [sins], your heavenly Father will also forgive you; but if you do not forgive others, neither will your Father forgive your trespasses" (Matthew 6:14–15). We cannot expect to be forgiven if we do not forgive. And who of us does not need to be forgiven? According to the New Testament, Jesus was more scathing in his rebuke of self-righteousness and hypocrisy than of any other form of sin. For a sinner to be unwilling to forgive the sins of others is to become unworthy of forgiveness. That is perhaps the strongest case to be made for forgiveness.

That case is pretty compelling in the situation we face. If the root of the president's sin is the disconnection between sex and loving commitment, his is a sin that in varying forms and degrees is widely shared throughout our culture. A very large number of people have violated their marriage vows—less than half the adult population, we may suppose, but still in the tens of millions. Who, among them, could without hypocrisy refuse to forgive the president? Who, among them, does not also feel a need for forgiveness, even if lucky enough not to have been subjected to public scrutiny?

But the essential sin is much more widely shared, even, by those who have never committed adultery. Sexual exploitation can occur even in the setting of a formally faithful, monogamous marriage. There are and always have been loveless marriages, but loveless marriages are not necessarily sexless. Moreover, cheap attitudes toward sex are very widely shared in this culture. That is obviously so of pornography; it is also true in the use of sexual appeal in mass media in general, including, of course, advertising. Jesus' further words in the Sermon on the Mount can be pondered: "You have heard that it was said, 'You shall not commit adultery.' But I say to you that everyone who looks at a woman with lust has already committed adultery with her in his heart" (Matthew 5:27–28). That is the "sin" that the straight-arrow former president Jimmy Carter famously confessed in an interview some years ago. What are we to make of it? Who has not had sexual fantasies, featuring sundry forms of "lust"? The number, expanding on Jesus' implied message, surely includes women as well as men! My guess is that the number of people who have committed the sin of "lusting in their hearts" approaches 100 percent of the human race!

Was Jesus placing an utterly impossible standard before us? Maybe so. It certainly has been true that numbers of people through history have been tormented by their inability to control their lustful thoughts and whose efforts to repress those thoughts have had damaging psychological consequences. Somehow I do not think Jesus was so much asking us to struggle against feelings that are built into our human nature as he was reinforcing the message about hypocrisy. Do not be so quick to condemn people for doing what you have *wanted* to do! Of course, neither is lust without love to be commended. Sexuality is a good gift to us when it is expressed through faithful love, and not when it is separated from and in conflict with real love. But given the reality of such sin, we should be slow to condemn and quick to forgive. That is the treatment we get from God, who is compassionate with us in our weaknesses.

More needs to be said about forgiveness, however. Even if it is true that we are all sinners who need to be forgiven, and even if we all should therefore be more willing to forgive, a forced kind of forgiveness may not be very healthy. Both pastors and professionals in the field of psychology are well aware of people who feel guilty about things they shouldn't feel guilty about and who, therefore, feel pressure to forgive too easily. For instance, a child who was sexually abused may carry extraordinary feelings of guilt well into adult life, even though the abuse was certainly not the child's fault. It can be very liberating to come to terms with such feelings, perhaps under the sensitive questioning of a therapist. Or a wife may feel that she is somehow at fault for the abusive behavior of her husband—or she may feel that at least she should be very "Christian" about it and continue to forgive him. For her (in spousal abuse it is usually the wife, not the husband, who is the victim), it can be liberating to discover that the abuse really is not her fault. Forgiveness itself can be an important part of one's liberation from abusive patterns—it can be a part of the letting go so one is no longer captive to the old abusive relationship. But in such situations genuine forgiveness is not something we can give solely because we feel guilty for not giving it. We must really want to forgive.

What, then, is the role of repentance? It is certainly a lot easier to forgive somebody who is genuinely contrite. Notice how people react after criminal trials. It seems to make a big difference whether or not the one who has been convicted shows remorse. The general tendency is to want to pile more punishment onto the remorseless evil-doer than the person who obviously regrets the harm he or she has done to others. An important part of the reason for this is that the crime itself has diminished the humanity of its victims and the public recognition of that diminishment by the perpetrator is a reaffirmation of what has been lost. In turn, the punishment of the unrepentant criminal is a statement by the community that the personhood of those who have been injured still matters to the rest of their fellow citizens.

Repentance is also important for the healing and moral growth of the wrongdoer—which at one time or another surely includes all of us. We cannot very well grow beyond the level of our wrongdoing until we confront it and resolve to change. That, again, cannot be contrived. We really have to believe that what we did was wrong. We must feel more than sincere regret that we got caught in the violation of a law and must now pay the consequences. Genuine repentance is recognition that we've done real harm. We have hurt people; a good that might have been has been damaged because of what we ourselves have done. We didn't have to do it. If we hadn't things would be better. But we did do it, and now things are worse. Put in theological terms, we have acted against love, and so we have hurt other people while frustrating God's loving purposes. That is what sin is, broadly speaking.

A classic prayer of confession says:

> We have left undone those things which we ought to have done; And we have done those things which we ought not to have done; And there is no health in us.

That prayer is appropriately repeated in public worship by a whole faith community because it aptly describes us all. Surely repentance helps to heal the wounded spirit of the sinner and to restore the brokenness of community. Similarly, the various twelve-step programs (dealing with alcoholism, drug abuse, sexual addiction, and overeating, for example) emphasize these points of repentance and seek to make amends, while finding religious support and help from others.

I have been asked numbers of times during this crisis how we can know that repentance is "genuine." I frankly don't know. I suspect that with all of us, repentance is clouded a bit by other things, and I know that it is a process by which we come to a deeper realization of the damage we have done. Sometimes we even discover that we have been repenting the wrong things and that our really serious sins are other than what we thought they were. In the end, the authenticity of one's repentance may be known only to God. In the meantime, we have our intuitions. Most pastors come to sense a faked repentance rather well, although we, too, can be fooled. More often, we can see that somebody is trying to repent and making some progress and needing some help. Perhaps that describes all of us, to some degree.

Still, it may be more important for us as individuals and sinners in such circumstances to ask whether we have a genuine prospect of forgiveness. I do not believe most people are capable of genuine repentance unless there is some light at the end of the tunnel, some likelihood that they will, in the end, be forgiven. We can regret that we have been caught. We can feel remorse or embarrassment in the face of the disapproval of the community. We can experience, with sadness, the harm we have done. But it still takes a measure of grace to be enabled to do the turnaround that repentance implies. We need love to be enabled to change. Paul exclaimed, "I do not do what I want, but I do the very thing I hate. . . . I can will what is right, but I cannot do it. For I do not do the good I want, but the evil I do not want is what I do" (Romans 7:15b,

18b–19). "Wretched man that I am," he continues, "Who will rescue me from this body of death?" (v. 24). For Christians, only the attractive power of God's grace in Jesus Christ will do it. The spiritual insight here may also find expression in other religious traditions. The heart of morality is in our response to love. It is not in the sheer force of willpower to obey moral or civil laws. Deep repentance is an act of recovered love.

That is why I have drawn in such stark terms the choice facing the nation between the way of repentance and forgiveness and the way of condemnation and punishment. The way out for the nation is not in condemning and punishing a president who lost his way. It is in broadly shared repentance over the broadly shared sin and moral growth through mutual forgiveness. Condemnation and punishment can sometimes tighten social control and foster conformity, but that is very far from true moral growth. True moral growth means growth toward wanting to be good and to do good for the sake of goodness. It does not mean doing and being good to avoid being condemned by others. Moral growth is growth in love.

How is it possible to love, to forgive? In the end, loving and forgiving lie in the deep realization that we ourselves have been loved to the bottom of our being. "We love," says the First Letter of John in the New Testament, "because he first loved us" (1 John 4:19). We can forgive because we have been forgiven. I suspect that the most unforgiving people are those who find it most difficult to receive love, for whatever reason. It helps a lot if that sense of being loved has religious roots. When we believe that God, the center and source of all being, really cares about us, that makes it so much easier to care about others. When we are most insecure religiously, caught up in a religious faith that emphasizes fear and punishment and wondering what we could ever do to earn God's favor, then it is natural for us to project those fears and insecurities on others. Instinctively we draw other people into the circle of insecurity we have woven about ourselves. Our condemnation of the sins of others is a way of dealing with our own sins, for which we can find no forgiveness.

This is why I find in the present national crisis a struggle by the nation to define its soul.

THE IMPORTANCE
OF SOCIAL DISCIPLINES

If this helps bring the ultimate issues into focus, it also raises many further questions. I will postpone several of these for the moment. But I must respond to one immediately: that is the question of whether or not love and forgiveness, though good and necessary in themselves, can create social havoc if we relax protections of law and the mechanisms of social control altogether. Is there not a need for social disciplines to protect people's well-being? There certainly is. In a public conversation with the head of the Southern Baptist Convention, I was asked what my attitude would be toward someone who stole my automobile. I might well be forgiving, at the spiritual level; indeed, I ought to be. But would I not want to do something to protect my automobile next time around?

Of course I would! A similar question was posed to me by a conservative member of Congress. He, too, concurred about the need for love and forgiveness. But, he asserted, actions have consequences. If the president of the United States is able to violate the law with impunity, what are we to say to all the people who are locked up in the nation's prisons? His question, however, implied erroneously that the president's misbehavior was the equivalent of the crimes that have sent people to prison, and it did not acknowledge the fact that not all known offenses are even prosecuted—much less punished.

Nevertheless these are serious questions, deserving thoughtful answers. Put in the language of love, they remind us of the importance of "tough love," or what Martin Luther referred to as the "strange work of love," by which he meant the need to do such things as using force to punish or restrain evil, not in violation of love but for the sake of love. Correcting a child may appear to the child to be unloving, but in fact it may be the most loving thing a parent can do. Catching and prosecuting criminals is, at least to them, an action that expresses the community's hostility. And yet it is an act of love for the community that is being protected and, quite possibly, an act of love for the criminal in restraining him or her from antisocial behavior. (I do not wish to imply that it is love that always inspires the execution of criminal laws, but only that it can be and should be.)

When asked by the congressman whether I didn't think there had to be "consequences" for wrongful behavior, I replied that there *already have been* consequences. Who could possibly conclude that the president had "gotten away" with the behavior? Is it not obvious that he has suffered massively and that everybody, young and old alike, would have to conclude that there have been painful consequences to his behavior? Has he not suffered much more than most people who have been involved in similar behavior? That certainly includes the sexual part of the charges against him. Most of the people who have violated their marriage vows have doubtless "gotten away with it," at least in the sense that the behavior has never been discovered, much less widely publicized. (Most probably have *not* "gotten away with it" on a spiritual level.) That seems also to have been true of a number of the president's predecessors.

Perhaps the same can be said of the truthfulness side. The president looked the country in the eye and said some things that were not true. It is an unresolved legal question whether he also said untrue things under oath in a legal deposition and in later testimony before a Washington grand jury. I am not a lawyer. I do not know, technically, if the case that he committed perjury is very strong. There is little doubt that he sought to conceal the extramarital sexual behavior as, I suppose, most people would. That does not justify his efforts, but his behavior is understandable. The question, then, is whether this kind and degree of dishonesty destroys the level of trust that is necessary for a chief executive to have in order to lead and to govern. In other words, should a consequence of his behavior be his removal from office? I will take this up later in the book, but a key issue remains whether the form of immorality—or even of illegality—has social, and not only personal, effects. And are any social effects serious enough to warrant removal?

I do not quite see it that way. Certainly the whole episode has not enhanced the level of trust. But the coverup, the dishonesty, was about wrongful personal behavior. It was not dishonesty about what is best for the nation that led people to do things contrary to their own and the nation's interests. It was not untruthfulness about matters of national policy and direction.

I am sufficiently acquainted with American history to know that there is not any U.S. president who has been absolutely truthful all the time—even the father of our country is no exception to that generalization. The great divide here, it seems to me, has been between those who have been utterly committed to the public good and who have been able to communicate that to the people honestly and well, and those whose communications and policies have been determined more by self-interest and the interests of well-placed elites. Most successful politicians cut corners to get into office, though not as much as cynics believe. But here the moral questions of truthfulness are not as clear-cut as we might wish. The issue is not that some politicians are absolutely truthful while others are basically dishonest. It is rather a question of more or less, a question of degree.

But have other politicians—including previous presidents of the United States—lied under oath, thereby violating the integrity of the laws they have sworn to uphold? So far as presidents are concerned, I don't know of any. But neither do I know of any who have been put under oath to answer embarrassing questions about their personal lives. And, presidents aside, how many perjury indictments are ever brought in situations like this? I do not wonder that the president invoked every available legalism to counter the barrage of legalism he had to confront. I say this not to justify his conduct, but to seek a better sense of proportion about it.

The question of forgiveness is paramount. Should President Clinton, or anybody in similar circumstances, be forgiven for such misbehavior? Remember again that we have all sinned and fallen short, and that we are all in need of forgiveness. Remember that forgiveness draws us toward a higher level of spiritual existence, a rediscovery of love as the center of moral life. Remember that particular punishments or sanctions must be in the service of love, not a replacement of love with an ethic of condemnation or vindictiveness. Remember that such sanctions must also be proportionate. Remember that God is finally the source of our own forgiveness and of the power to be forgiving.

I will reflect in the last chapter on the way out of the situation we face. But I wish to stress again that there can be no moral resolution in the absence of love.

— 4 —

The Nation's Uncertainty

When the history of this period is written, I am sure that historians will continue to shake their heads in amazement. Despite the shock waves of sensationalism and the biting criticism of most of the nation's news commentators and many other influential people, the public opinion polls have continued to support the president's performance in office and to reject calls for his removal. By large margins. Sometimes new revelations have actually increased the support, not decreased it—as occurred in the days following the release of the Starr Report and in the aftermath of the broadcasting of the president's grand jury testimony. For instance, on September 14, following widespread publication of the Starr Report, *USA Today* reported that 66 percent of those surveyed opposed impeachment, 62 percent opposed resignation, and the president's job performance approval was at 64 percent—slightly higher than in recent weeks. Ironically, these poll results were published in the same edition of the newspaper that contained an editorial calling for his resignation.

At the same time, public confidence in him as a moral leader or a person to be trusted had declined. In that same poll, the newspaper reported, "only 37 percent expressed a positive opinion of the man" and 54 percent indicated they did not respect him. Similar poll results have been published week after week throughout the crisis, with little change, from the beginning of the crisis in January, 1998. There are small variations among the different polls, but basically that has been the picture. Following the release and broadcast of videotapes of the president's grand jury testimony on September 21, a *New York Times*/CBS poll found 66 percent of those surveyed approved of the president's job performance and only 29 percent supported impeachment hearings (published in the *New York Times*, September 25, 1998). Large majorities expressed criticism of congressional handling of the crisis; even larger majorities were critical of the Office of the Independent Counsel. Later, after the House of Representatives voted to launch a formal impeachment investigation, a *Washington Post*/ABC News survey found that the number of respondents approving of President Clinton's performance as president had risen to 67 percent—and 62 percent indicated they disapproved of the way Republicans in Congress were handling the impeachment issue (*Washington Post*, October 12, 1998).

What are we to make of this?

The Role of
Intervening Elites

To sort this out we need to understand how influence is exerted in a democratic society. We tend to think that public opinion is formed from a direct relationship between top national leadership and the broad base of the population. Sometimes that is so, for instance, in situations where everybody is more or less simultaneously influenced by the same events or personalities. When Winston Churchill made his memorable appeals to the British nation during the Battle of Britain, it was the top political leader directly influencing the whole nation to sacrifice and endure. Franklin D. Roosevelt's "fireside chats" had something of the same effect. In the television era, presidents and other top leaders have at some times been able to gain direct support in that kind of way.

But patterns of influence are usually more complicated. Standing between the top leaders and the broad mass of the public are many influential people whose views seriously affect the attitudes the people will take. We are all greatly influenced by others. Nobody could possibly know enough about the issues facing us so that he or she can make informed decisions about them all; even our day-to-day opinions are largely determined by the views of people we respect. That does not mean we turn to the same people for everything. When it comes to personal medical issues, we will usually take a doctor's informed opinion at face value. That does not mean we will seek the doctor's advice on our business decisions or political attitudes. On political matters we are likely to be influenced by respected commentators, including familiar voices on television news programs, columnists and editorial writers, and the authors of influential books, as well as by politicians we trust. On questions involving deeper moral or spiritual meaning, pastors, theologians, and ethicists can be influential, particularly within their own religious communities, but sometimes with a wider public. The process can be quite subtle. Sometimes public opinion shifts dramatically between the time an event occurs and after the "influentials" have finished analyzing it. It is as though a digestion process occurs, and influential commentators help us to process the events we have seen or read about as raw news.

It is probably a good thing that such a process occurs. Our first and immediate impressions may not be well thought out. We may need help. In fact, the worst moments in twentieth-century political history have generally occurred when demagogues like Hitler and Mussolini succeeded in stampeding whole societies. The intervening elites in the press, universities, and churches were either bought off or their opposition was crushed. There have been moments of such demagoguery in America, of course. One thinks of nineteenth-century nativism, when demagogues spewed out hatred of foreign immigrants, Roman Catholics, and Jews, who were as a result then treated unfairly, and one thinks of mid-twentieth-century McCarthyism. American democracy has generally weathered such storms because of the checks and balances built into our system of government and because of the rich fabric of intellectual and religious institutions with which the country has been blessed. Aristotle's chief argument against democracy was its vulnerability to demagoguery. In the case of America—and many other democracies in the contemporary world—democracy has succeeded largely because of the rich fabric of intervening elites.

So what has happened with the intervening elites in the present crisis situation? The most visible opinion leaders—that is, the ones with highest visibility in the mass media—have been among the president's most severe critics. Across the country some one hundred newspapers—mostly small, but including a few major ones like the *Philadelphia Inquirer* and the *Atlanta Journal-Constitution*—have called for the president's resignation. And in editorials, even moderate to liberal papers such as the *Washington Post* and the *New York Times*, while stopping short of calling for his removal from office, have expressed what amounts to unmitigated contempt.

Among columnists and other influential writers, one would perhaps expect this same treatment from a George Will or a William Bennett. Such writers have been opposed to President Clinton all along. But his critics have also included the more moderate voices, such as David Broder of the *Washington Post* and Clarence Page of the *Chicago Tribune*. Major newsmagazines, like *Time* and *Newsweek*, have had a distinctly negative tone, even in articles designed as straight news analysis. *Newsweek* columnist Jonathan Alter wrote that "the greatest surprise in this whole story is the ongoing gap between the elites—who now almost uniformly despise Clinton—and the people, who have stuck with him so far." My own fairly wide reading suggests that Alter has overstated the negativism of "the elites." There are influential persons in the media (such as Haynes Johnson of the *Washington Post* and Russell Baker of the *New York Times*), influential political figures (such as Congressmen John Lewis and Barney Frank), influential media personalities (such as Garrison Keillor), and religious leaders (such as Reverend Joan Brown Campbell, General Secretary of the National Council of Churches, and others who gathered for the White House prayer breakfast) who are supportive of the president. Still, there is no question that a very large number of journalistic commentators have condemned the president.

In light of the generally unfavorable cast of such opinion leaders, why has public opinion been affected so little? One would certainly have expected otherwise. Even the journalists, as evidenced by Alter's comment, have been surprised by this. Howard Kurtz, writing in the *Washington Post*, reported that "sizable majorities still tell pollsters they approve of the president's job performance and oppose impeachment or resignation," commenting that "the contrast with the media's collective sense of betrayal has never been starker."

WHY THE LOSS
OF INFLUENCE?

Part of the explanation may be that whole layers of opinion leadership are not so visible. The major media—

television, newspapers, newsmagazines—are highly visible by definition. We do not know yet (at least I do not) what has been going on with more local leadership. For instance, someday somebody will study what the nation's clergy have been saying in their pulpits during the crisis. Some, no doubt, have been happy enough to ignore it altogether. I suspect, though, that many a sermon has been preached about moral aspects of the crisis. We do not yet know what has been said. It would also be interesting to ask, in the regular polls, who (as distinct from what) has most influenced the respondents in arriving at their views. I am not aware of studies of that sort, although they could be revealing as we attempt to gauge the patterns of opinion leadership. One clue may be in some polling data that reveals negative attitudes toward the press—an explicit indication that that form of elite influence is not much affecting public opinion. But further studies would be helpful as we try to measure the relationships between the public and the intervening elites.

In the meantime, any number of views have been offered to explain the gap.

Prior to the release of the Starr Report, and then prior to the airing of videotapes of the president's grand jury testimony, it was often said (especially by journalists critical of the president) that it was just a matter of time. As soon as the Report, and later the videotapes, were digested by the public we could expect a rapid shift in public opinion. It hasn't worked that way.

Instead, those moments of truth seem to have had the opposite effect. The more the public was "educated," the less it seemed to support the president's removal—although the personal respect percentages went down. Indeed, the fact that the poll data have remained so constant over a period of many months suggests that it is not just a question of time.

It has also been argued that the data reflect satisfaction, not with the president, but with the general prosperity of the times. It was not about Paula Jones but Dow Jones! If the economy were to go bad one could expect the president's ratings to follow suit. That is a tempting argument. But, during August and September 1998, the economic situation was exacerbated by economic crisis in Asia and sharp declines in U.S. stock markets. That, too, did not seem to affect the president's ratings. Some may even have blamed the economic difficulties on their perception that the president was being harassed.

Then, of course, there is the feeling among some cultural conservatives that the president's high job approval ratings mean that public standards of morality have become debased and that issues of sexual morality are not very important to many people—all the more reason, among those critics, to blame the president for the effect he has had on the country. It is, in fact, striking that in many of the media's street interviews people can be heard to say that this is all about the president's private sex life and that is none of our business. On September 11 (the day the Starr Report was made public), while waiting my turn to appear on *Larry King Live*, I was struck by this very disconnect. Waiting with me in a hospitality room were several media pundits and members of Congress. Most of them were critical of the president, and a number of them considered the Starr Report to be evidence of potential impeachability. As we waited, CNN was reporting street corner interviews with ordinary people in places as separated geographically and culturally as Boston, Massachusetts and Peoria, Illinois. I expected the interviews to reflect the kinds of criticisms of the president I was hearing in the room. But they did not. Almost *all* of the randomly interviewed people were critical, not of the president but of the investigations and the media's coverage. A number of the people interviewed spoke of this as an intrusion into the president's private life. So the cultural conservatives may be right in saying that private sexual morality does not appear to be all that important to many people.

The typical response of critics has been that the issue is actually about possible perjury and obstruction of justice, rather than sexual peccadillos. The sexual misbehavior may be the more disgusting to many people, but the perjury and obstruction of justice, if proven, are crimes. Still, the view of many ordinary people seems to be that the attempt to conceal embarrassing sexual behavior, whatever its technical legal significance, is an understandable preservation of privacy that should never have been invaded in the first place. From that perspective, it all still comes back to sex, and the president's sexual behavior ought not to be subject to public investigation.

I am not quite sure how to evaluate this viewpoint. Insofar as it means that there are many people who do not consider sexual morality important, that is disturbing.

Perhaps it is more disturbing than surprising, for American culture is discernibly less concerned about sexual morality today than it was a generation or two ago. But sexual morality really does matter, not because we ought to be more puritanical but because sexual behavior can be harmful when it is not expressed in a loving and committed relationship. That is obviously true of sexual exploitation or violence; I believe it is also true of more casual forms of promiscuity and adultery. One does not have to be moralistic or self-righteous to see that monogamous, committed love is the best setting for sexual activity, and that there are moral risks in looser behavior. I suppose a certain percentage of those who keep the president's poll ratings high is made up of people who are not much concerned about that. It seems clear, at least to me, that those people are not going to change their views about this anytime soon. If they do change their minds, it will not be to accommodate a moralistic approach to sex. Perhaps it will be in the direction of a deeper ethic of love. I hope so. Meanwhile many others who do object to the president's sexual behavior still seem also to feel that this is not their business.

Doubtless a certain percentage of the president's continuing supporters are prompted more by political motivations than anything else. He represents the attitudes and policies they support, so they are naturally reluctant to see him removed from office. Even though his replacement would be a vice president whose views are parallel to his, the effect of his removal would be to diminish the strength of those policies and attitudes in American public life. Of course, the other side of that coin is the possibility that many of the president's most persistent critics have never supported his public leadership in the first place. For them, the removal of this president from office has ideological or partisan advantages–even though for the most partisan it would carry the prospect of having to run against an incumbent president in the year 2000. The polling data, broken down into party affiliation, clearly show much greater support for the president among members of his own party than among Republicans, although it is striking that a substantial number of Republicans also do not want to see him forced from office.

QUESTIONS OF PROPORTION

While those factors are at work in the formation of public opinion, I believe there may be some deeper considerations. There is no question that the public, as a whole, has wanted the issue to just go away—even as there continues to be a large measure of public fascination with it. There is also no question, at least in my mind, that millions of people have been in grief over the situation and circumstances. That may be hard to understand. But remember that Americans invest a great deal of psychic ownership in the presidency. The president, as chief of state, embodies the meaning and values of the nation, and most of us consider our membership (citizenship) in the nation to be an important part of our identity. One does not have to be a super-nationalist to feel the weight of that. We are quite prepared to make due allowances for the flawed humanity of our chief executive, but the holder of that office is still an embodiment of national values and purposes.

One might suppose, in light of this, that it is an ominous sign when public opinion shows much lower support for the president as person than for the president as competent executive leader. It is commonplace among the president's critics to hear the complaint that he has demeaned the office and that the nation wants and deserves to have a president it can be proud of. Have the more than 60 percent of the people who continue to support him in office been inconsistent about this?

Maybe they have, to some extent. The negative attitudes toward the president's personal character clearly reflect that. And yet, one remembers the enormous effectiveness with which President Clinton has rallied the nation in disasters such as the Oklahoma City bombing. Nor can one forget how well he has reached the public in the more routine appeals he has made in behalf of social security, public education, public health (including the effort to stop tobacco use by children and young people), and the ongoing struggles against racism, terrorism, and violence. There have been less successful moments in the Clinton presidency, including the failure of health care reform and the resolution of the "gays in the military" question. But on the whole, there is much evidence of a very effective presidency.

I wonder if the public at large may have a fuller understanding of this president's character than many of the media pundits. Elites may be inclined to define a leader entirely by his observable flaws. The public may take better account of the president's many positives. Most people do not like his misbehavior. Many are in fact outraged by it. But at the same time, they can see much that remains attractive. That is evidenced by the sadness one often encounters in conversations about the president's difficulties. People might not be quite so grief-stricken about this if they didn't, at some level, really *like* this man. If he were viewed simply as a scoundrel who had managed to trick his way into office, a large majority of the people would long since have said, "Be gone and good riddance." But that is not the message of the polls.

I have a theory about this. It is that people respond best to a leader, not when he or she is flamboyant or charismatic, but when they sense that the leader really cares about them. Flawed though the leader may be, either in his or her personal life or in matters of judgment, it matters a lot whether or not that leader is thoroughly devoted to the public good. It matters if the leader is sensitive to people, if he or she is capable of really listening to them and taking serious account of their views and their aspirations. A certain amount of opinion is very dismissive of the president at such points. But my guess is that a majority of citizens are not so cynical. So the question is whether or not the public may have a more balanced view, a greater sense of proportion about the man and what is at stake in the situation, than do many of the elites. That is at least worth pondering.

Even if I have overstated this point, there is another aspect to the question of proportion. The people of this country value the stability of its institutions very highly. Setting aside the results of a presidential election by means of impeachment has been broached in a serious way only twice before in the nation's history. My guess is that comparatively few people like the idea of impeachment used as a routine political weapon, by means of which elections can be nullified—and they fear that such is the case here. The constitutional test is that a president can be removed from office only if "high crimes and misdemeanors" have been committed. That sounds like a very exacting standard. What does it mean? Former president Gerald Ford, when in the House of Representatives, remarked that that language means whatever Congress says it means. Literally that is so, for there is no appeal from a congressional decision on these matters. And yet the sense I have is that the public at large wants the language to mean offenses that are very grave and not minor or technical violations of the law. Opinions on that can vary greatly. On the whole, how-ever, the public seems prepared to grant more leeway than many of the intervening elites appear to approve. One of the president's more persistent critics has been William Kristol, editor of the *Weekly Standard*. While he considers public opinion to be wrong in its continued support of the president, Kristol still can write, "It's important that people in the media who are convinced they are absolutely right stop and think whether there's a lesson to be learned from public opinion. It *should* be difficult to convince people to be for impeachment."

THE NEED TO UPHOLD
MORAL STANDARDS

Uncertain as the nation seems to be about all this, we must note the persistent uneasiness about the president's self-acknowledged misbehavior. He didn't behave the way the country wants its president to behave. It can be understood, humanly speaking, but it can hardly be approved. I have spoken already of the importance of the connection between sexual expression and loving commitment. I believe most people would agree to the importance of that standard, even when they have a hard time living by it.

In view of the vast publicity that has been given to the details of the president's misbehavior, there may be a felt need to mark that off, somehow, as unacceptable. I am intrigued by the discussion of a congressional reprimand of some sort as a way to accomplish this, although it is interesting that, following the broadcast of the president's grand jury testimony, a small majority in some public opinion polls even rejected the idea of a congressional censure. I am not sure how to interpret that. I suspect that the public would welcome some way of registering the unacceptability of his conduct so the country can move on.

ATTITUDES TOWARD THE
INVESTIGATIVE PROCESS

Before leaving this chapter, we should perhaps remind ourselves of the widespread unhappiness with the way in which the story became public: the years of relentless investigation, the tape recording of Monica Lewinsky's telephone conversations, the release of everything—including the most salacious details—to the public. Public reactions against all of this have doubtless played an important part in the continued support for the president. The public's sense of fairness may have been offended. In its evaluation of the great moral drama occupying the nation, the public may feel that insufficient attention has been given to the moral shortcuts, even misbehavior, of those who have pursued the president. That leads to questions we now need to explore.

— 5 —

Misgivings about the Process

Following services at Foundry on the last Sunday in January, which President and Mrs. Clinton attended, I was interviewed by a reporter from the *New York Daily News*. She had been a part of the cluster of reporters who generally appear when the president is in attendance, and she had lingered after the service. She was reassuring and conveyed the impression that she fully understood my views and would report them in a moderate, responsible way. And she did just that in the article. But I had forgotten the sensationalist style of that newspaper, and I was chagrined to read the next day's headline: "Prez' minister blasts independent counsel." For it had not been my intention to "blast" anybody!

In fact, a critical analysis of the four-year operation of the Office of the Independent Counsel is even beyond the scope of this book. I am less concerned here about the details of that operation and more concerned about the broad effects the emerging crisis has had and will

have on the moral state of the nation. But the investigative process and its coverage in the media have had
such effects, so we cannot ignore them.

I confess that I have had serious misgivings about the
investigative process, even though there is merit to the
idea of having a totally independent agency investigate
possible wrongdoing by a high official of government. If
such an investigation were to be carried out by an agency
whose head is appointed by the president, the public
might wonder about its objectivity. To gain public
confidence in the integrity of an investigation, it must be
pursued by officials whose objectivity and freedom from
personal or partisan bias is beyond reproach. The theory
is that an independently appointed counsel would be
more objective than the U.S. Department of Justice, since
the head of that agency, the Attorney General, is
appointed by the president. In fact, the blatant attempts
by the Nixon White House to control the Justice Department's investigations of Watergate were largely responsible for the legislation providing for independent
counsels. Both the reality and the appearance of
independence and objectivity were rightly considered
important to preserve the integrity of investigations.

Some of my misgivings about the present process are
exactly at that point. The special counsel, Kenneth Starr,
had been a high official in the administration that
President Clinton had defeated in 1992. Whether fairly or
not, his relationships with Clinton's ideological foes, such
as Pat Robertson, Jerry Falwell, and the Rutherford
Institute, raised widespread questions about his ability to

maintain the necessary levels of objectivity. These relationships alone would not be cause for too much concern if the actual investigative process had proceeded with due regard for fairness, discretion, and proportion. I am not alone in questioning if it has.

Many people wonder about the investigative procedures that led to President Clinton's being charged with perjury. The use of Linda Tripp's secret (and possibly illegal) tape recordings of conversations with Monica Lewinsky strikes one as the sort of evidence-gathering that should be reserved for truly heinous crimes, not to expose two people's sexual misbehavior and their embarrassed efforts to cover it up. The charges emanating from this are not about sexual misbehavior, of course, but about perjury, subornation of perjury, and conspiracy. These are serious charges, legally and morally, and the sexual misbehavior itself is morally, though not legally, serious as well. It is not my purpose to go into the merits of the charges, but rather to ask, do we want to encourage such forms of investigation?

There is also the related question of proportion. Are the charges here of such magnitude as to warrant prosecution? It is often said that no one should be above the law, not even the president of the United States. I hope everyone agrees with that. But one must remember that prosecutors have wide discretion in deciding what kinds of offenses are serious enough to prosecute and under what circumstances. I have real questions about   whether an ordinary person, found to have engaged in extramarital sexual activity and to have lied about it under oath in a civil case that was thrown out by the judge   for reasons unrelated to that person's testimony, would have been subjected to all this investigation, much less actual prosecution. If that sounds like an excuse for the president's conduct, I do not intend it in that way. I do not even mean to say that the moral and legal offenses are not worthy of further notice. I do mean to say that the independent counsel may not have been sufficiently objective and fair.

In justifying the process, one jurist is reputed to have said that it is just good standard prosecutorial practice to go after the target with every legal weapon at hand. The adversarial system in American law is constructed on that basis: If the prosecution lawyers and the defense lawyers each give it all they've got, then truth and fairness will emerge in court. That may often work in the legal system (though it often doesn't, too), but I am troubled by the implication that it is a special prosecutor's job, once appointed, to bring the president down if he can. Was that really the intention of the statute? My concerns here go far beyond the legal niceties. What would the long-term effect be in American public life for the notion to take hold that a president can be subjected to the closest scrutiny, year after year, by a well-financed team of highly competent lawyers and investigators whose mission is to find incriminating information? I am concerned about the sheer *political power* inherent in such a position.

The power of the independent counsel's position is illustrated by his ability to subpoena large numbers of witnesses. Very little restraint or sensitivity has been shown in the way this power has been exercised, with Monica Lewinsky's college friends and mother called to testify, along with scores of other people who had any relationship or potential knowledge of the situation. Can you imagine such a process being mounted against an ordinary citizen in like circumstances? Even members of the Secret Service were required to testify, despite their serious professional objections. Those officers, sworn to protect the president and, if necessary, to give their own lives to do so, must remain in the closest proximity to him and his family. I have observed this, myself, when President Clinton has attended church. The agents are discreet, but they are very professional, very thorough, and very close. Not infrequently, they are close enough to hear conversations. Does a president need to guard every word when an agent is hovering close by? Much of the conversation may be political, including information that could be sought after by a president's political opponents. Should a president have to fear that the protective agents could be made to testify? The Secret Service's own resistance was based on the fear that future presidents, perceiving this as a vulnerability, might keep their distance from the agents in some situations. A court allowed the special prosecutor to proceed with this, but I question the wisdom of it. When Starr pushed so hard to secure such testimony—and that of other close associates of the president whose relationships might well have been considered privileged—I had to wonder if we have a special prosecutor who really wants to "get" this president.

I had other misgivings. Why was it deemed necessary to publish all the lurid sexual details in the Report and its appendices? Many have strongly objected to the inclusion of such material, especially given its repetitive nature and the exclusion of exculpatory evidence. It became downright embarrassing as the television networks competed to get the Report out first, hastily reading the document as it was downloaded off the Internet. Material that would have been banned from prime time television was paraded in broad daylight under the guise of informing the public. And one congressman suggested that if people did not want to read it, they could turn off their televisions. What stand will he take on the regulation of pornography on television and the Internet?

Was this so necessary? Some argued that the detail was necessary in order to show that the president lied in his deposition in the Jones case and later before the grand jury. I have read through much of this material, and you don't have to be a lawyer to encounter the redundancies. Was that necessary for legal reasons? I seriously doubt it. This Report was identified by the Special Prosecutor as a report to Congress, but it clearly was intended to inflame public opinion.

The issue of fairness is raised again over the fact that the White House was not given the courtesy of an advance copy of the Report. Why not? Richard Nixon had been afforded that courtesy twenty-five years earlier, as was Newt Gingrich, the Speaker of the House, more recently. The best excuse for that was that it had to be delivered to Congress immediately, lest the White House somehow tie it up in court. That sounds more like a political calculation than a legal one. Even so, why couldn't a copy of the Report have gone to the White House at exactly the same time as Congress? I believe that the desire was to let the Report affect public opinion without a response from the White House, at least for a couple of days.

I do not know whether or not I was the only one in the country who drew the conclusion from these events that the Report presented a weak case, not a strong one, for impeachment. If the special prosecutor had a strong case—an open-and-shut, clear case of "high crimes and misdemeanors"—it would not have been *necessary* to do these things. Why not let the president and his legal staff have a thorough look at the whole thing? If it were a clear case, no rebuttal on their part would have mattered much.

I have spoken of these as misgivings about the process. Lurking beneath all this are fundamental attitudes and values. The process just doesn't ring true to the attitudes of decency and fairness that are important to this country when we are at our best. Much of my criticism hinges on the spirit in which the process has been carried out. I think we can do better than this as a country.

CIVILITY IN POLITICS

My concerns go beyond the present situation and events, beyond my pastoral concern for the president and his family, to concerns for our country. A great deal is at stake in this case that will ultimately affect public life.

Longtime members of Congress acknowledge that the

trend in that institution—and elsewhere in American politics—has been toward partisan and mean-spirited behavior. To be sure, there has always been a good deal of meanness in politics. There have been periods in history that have arguably been worse than this one. During the early part of the nineteenth century, for instance, congress- men sometimes literally engaged in fistfights. On some notable occasions, high government officials fought duels to the death. One of the greatest of the original American "founders," Alexander Hamilton, was killed in a duel by Vice President Aaron Burr in 1804. In 1838 Congressman William J. Graves of Kentucky killed Congressman Jonathan Cilley of Maine in a duel. That event finally stirred the country to action on dueling. (A Foundry Church predecessor of mine, Reverend Henry Slicer— also chaplain of the U.S. Senate—preached a stirring sermon against dueling and helped bring that form of barbarism to an end.) The struggle over slavery brought further political incivilities, and there have been other waves of meanness in public life. Maybe that is a recurrent danger in a democratic society in which real issues of power are determined by debates and elections. If so, people of good will must continue to encourage greater mutual respect and more restraint in the conduct of political battles.

What I fear in this regard is that one result of the Starr Report will be to encourage political parties in the future to take advantage of their positions of power to engage in dragnet searches for flaws and misbehaviors in their opponents, not just to influence the public prior to elections (which is bad enough) but to intimidate political adversaries with threats of criminal prosecution. The power to determine who the special prosecutors will be and the power to use the results of investigations politically can have a very chilling effect on public life. As I said in one of those September sermons, I worry about a growing tendency in politics, not just to defeat opponents but to destroy them. The struggle for political power is not bad in itself, for it is the ongoing contest over which policies will ultimately prevail. There has traditionally been the understanding that if one loses on one bill in Congress or in one election there will always be another opportunity, another election, in which to win. But if each contest is viewed as an all-or-nothing battle, and if political survival itself is always on the line, then there is not much room for dialogue and accommodation.

Suppose, for instance, that President Clinton were to be forced from office through the use of procedures and processes widely perceived by citizens to be unfair and against the wishes of large numbers of people—perhaps even a substantial majority of the people. What kind of bitterness would that unleash in America? Some people might be turned off by the political process, contributing further cynicism to an already too-cynical public. Others, including political opponents, might thirst for revenge. Sooner or later their turn for vengeance would also come. In the end, the constructive political process could fall victim to personal political agendas and the public civil debate might be badly weakened. So I have misgivings about where this process might lead.

My misgivings are not diminished by the extent to

which the process truly has been fueled by the resourceful collaboration of the president's most bitter enemies. How sad that his flawed behavior afforded them an opening. But their use of that opening can further deepen the incivilities of public life. I have been struck by the number of judgmental letters I have received about President Clinton that condemn the president's behavior while also condemning his political views. For such people, the president's problems must appear as a splendid opportunity to settle other kinds of scores.

Public life does not have to be this way. While periods of incivility have dotted our nation's history, so have times of grace and decency. The bipartisan cooperation during World War II typifies what I mean. Wendell Willkie, who had run a vigorous but unsuccessful campaign against President Franklin Roosevelt in 1940, then worked closely with Roosevelt as an unofficial emissary. Senators George McGovern and Robert Dole cooperated in the creation of the Food Stamp program. Even President Richard Nixon reached out to his ideological opponent Senator Ted Kennedy after the Chappaquiddick tragedy. There is grace in such political relationships, reminding us that we all belong to the same country and that our interest in its well-being—and that of the world—should transcend the immediate struggles.

When I spoke earlier of the nation defining its soul, in choosing between the spirit of the prayer breakfast and that of the Starr Report, I had something like this in mind. Of course we must be concerned about upholding the law, as the Starr Report purports to do. But the law ultimately functions in the service of a healthy society of people who care about one another and about the public good. It certainly is not the case that society exists for the sake of the law, not to mention for the sake of legalism.

To some, virtues like love and forgiveness may seem too soft, too accepting, and out of place in politics. But translated into the political disciplines of mutual respect and willingness to compromise for the greater good, love and forgiveness are the very essence of a healthy democratic society. Without these disciplines and these virtues, law loses its point and its power. Politicians need first to find love and forgiveness in their own lives, so their public life is not just a constant effort to shore up their own self-esteem through the exercise of power and by receiving the support of large numbers of people. But even the spiritually secure leader will not always have an easy time of it in being a person of grace in the public arena. Mutual respect and compromise can run counter to the immediate demands of party loyalty and public pressures. I do not pretend that this does not entail a good deal of personal struggle, political artfulness, and sometimes exquisite timing. But that must be the agenda for public leaders who wish their legacy to be the moral growth and health of the whole society.

We can find a touch of irony in the publication of another book by the conservative politician William J. Bennett, widely known as the editor of *The Book of Virtues*. His new book is from start to finish an almost unrelieved attack on the president's character, with scarcely a word of acknowledgment of the accomplishments and graces of his nearly six years in the presidency. Bennett overlooked a whole other side of the president's character and contributions to American life, despite his earlier support for some of Clinton's policies. Even what it did say was not altogether accurate—at least I felt personally misrepresented in the book's remarks about me. But the irony, to me, was for this arbiter of virtue to have so neglected in his book the most important virtue of all—love!

Of course, having raised the issue of the Starr Report and Bill Bennett's impartiality and fairness, as well as that of the other voices of like spirit, I must say more. Their concern about lowered standards of sexual morality is a message that needs to be heard—but it needs to be heard in the context of love or it completely loses its point. It cannot simply be a message of having and obeying standards for their own sake. Sexual moral standards are there for the sake of a much greater good; standards are for the sake of love. Their concern about law is likewise important; we are, and must be, a nation of law. But law, too, loses its point if it is not practiced in the context of a society of mutual caring in which a sense of proportion and a certain amount of common sense help us understand what the law is there to serve.

Such points may help us grasp a major distinction about sin. We should be opposed to every form of sin, of course. But if one had to choose the lesser of the evils, it might be better to choose the sin that is based on weakness rather than the sin that is an expression of malice.

I do not want to have to make such a choice. But I think I know the difference.

CONCERNS ABOUT THE MEDIA

This has not been journalism's finest hour. That opinion applies to both print and broadcast forms of communication. The tone of the reporting that persisted after January 1998 was prefigured by the behavior of major network news figures who were in Cuba covering the pope's visit in late January when the Clinton/Lewinsky story first broke. The pope's visit represented an important potential breakthrough in the troubled recent history of that country and in its relationship with the United States. As the story broke, the network anchors left the papal visit flatfooted and raced back to the United States to cover the more sensational domestic events. I am sure each of them would defend their action as recognizing what would be, to the American public, the more newsworthy story. But the pope's visit was of great historical importance, and there was nothing about the Clinton story that the network news organizations could not have handled without the presence of their anchors on U.S. soil. But this lack of judgment was just the beginning. For days, rumor built upon rumor. Major news organizations, including some of those of highest reputation, vied to be first with late-breaking developments. Unnamed sources were quoted freely; sometimes stories were based upon but one such unnamed source. Readers could not form intelligent opinions on the basis of the credibility or lack thereof of the sources. Along the way, some stories had to be retracted, but that did not slow the media down.

Some journalists were troubled by this; many apparently

were not. My purpose here is not to criticize particular journalists, articles, or programs. It is to share my misgivings about broader trends in the American media, as evidenced by the way this story proceeded. Two things especially come to my mind.

The first is to notice how competitive news gathering has become. I am sure the television news anchors who rushed home from Cuba would be quick to say that they would lose their competitive advantage if others were covering the emerging story with their "top guns" and their own networks were not. Hastening into print or on the air with late-breaking developments, even if it means abandoning traditional journalistic standards, can seem necessary at the moment in order to preserve the image of being first, best, or most complete with the news. News gathering in our society has always been somewhat competitive, of course—for at least the past century or so. But changes in economics and technology affect the climate in which journalism operates.

Around the turn of the century, when "yellow journalism" got its name, the world of newspaper publishing was highly competitive. News barons like William Randolph Hearst built journalistic empires on sensationalism. Even cities of moderate size had two, three, or more daily newspapers, with evening as well as morning editions. With that kind of competition, the more sensational the headlines, the more papers were sold. But the number of papers gradually receded, as the more successful forced the less competitive out of business. Evening papers disappeared, in part because of competition from television news and changes in employment and lifestyles. Sensationalism was much reduced and in many cases abandoned. Newspapers like the *Washington Post*, the *New York Times*, and the *Los Angeles Times* survived and earned reputations as highly responsible sources of news. Network television came down to three major news outlets: CBS, NBC, and ABC. They were competitive, of course, but each could count on major shares of the television market and each had a reputation for dependability.

In recent years technology has brought us full circle. Major newspapers can be printed and distributed in various locations beyond their home cities, so local papers in many cities find themselves competing with the *New York Times* and other major papers—and vice versa. Similar things have happened with television. With the development of cable and satellite television, there were no longer technical limits on the numbers of assignable channels. CNN emerged as a global giant, bringing news around the clock from around the world. NBC came on with MSNBC; then there was the Fox cable news channel, and others followed. Meanwhile, the Internet was opening up totally new possibilities with totally unregulated—and sometimes totally unrestrained—forms of news and gossip transmission. If a Boston or Chicago paper early in this century was in a highly competitive environment, that was nothing to the current scene with multiple forms of news transmission in a twenty-four-hour news cycle. There is one aspect of this that I have experienced firsthand since the crisis began: the cable networks have to fill all those hours with *something!* On occasion, I have found myself being that "something."

The inevitable effect of this highly competitive environment has been to lower journalistic standards and, as happened earlier in our history, to sensationalize the news. How could it have been otherwise?

But there is a second thing about the media's coverage of the story that one begins to notice. It has, I believe, more to do with the self-image and professional conceptions of the journalists themselves. Ever since Watergate and news coverage of the Vietnam War, the press has given major attention to the exposure of errors, hypocrisies, cover-ups, crimes, and flaws of people in public life. The Woodward and Bernstein saga made an indelible imprint on the profession. Those enterprising journalists demonstrated that certain events and corruptions needed exposing . . . that it was possible for honest reporters to get at the truth and for courageous publishers to print their stories. That, of course, is good as far as it goes. Public servants *do* need to have watchdogs. If the public is to participate responsibly in self-government, it has to be informed. The searchlight of truth can render an absolutely indispensable service to society. An honest and free press can help us all "walk in the light."

Still, I believe there is room for misgivings. I am troubled, not by the self-understanding of journalists, but by their excess and by their so easily identifying "truth" with "facts," as though the two are exactly the same thing. There obviously is a relationship between fact and truth, but the exposure of facts alone does not constitute truth. Indeed, it is possible to be entirely honest in the use of facts as we construct a broadly untruthful picture. An extreme example may help make the point. Suppose a reporter were to attend one of these gigantic Washington, D.C., demonstrations attended by hundreds of thousands of like-minded people, united by some common purpose. Suppose that on the outskirts of this mass event there were twenty or thirty counterdemonstrators, deeply opposed to that common purpose. If the reporter devoted most of his or her attention to the twenty or thirty, while neglecting the hundreds of thousands, he or she could be very factual—and very dishonest. Similarly a network newscast can hone in on particular faces in particular ways. Given the vividness of television, what those faces say is what defines the event for many. It is a question of how the face is selected.

I have also experienced this myself. I am seldom interviewed for only a minute or two. Indeed, most taped television interviews last fifteen or twenty minutes. But typically, only about eight or ten seconds of that interview will be used, if any is used at all. Given my own experience, when I see a brief statement by some prominent figure, I just assume that she or he was actually on camera for a much longer time and that the editors have decided what is to be used to fit the story. It is all "factual," but everything depends on which facts have been selected to convey the total story.

There is no way out of this, of course. And I have usually concurred with journalists' choice of quotes from their interviews with me. But in the handling of news in the highly competitive environment of network news and newspapers and given the new journalistic standard of exposing hidden flaws, the overall picture can be distorted.

In a thoughtful "Observer" column in the *New York Times* (October 9, 1998), Russell Baker raised serious questions about the media's preoccupation with sex in the coverage of the Clinton/Lewinsky story. Referring to his earlier years as a reporter, Baker commented:

> I was untroubled by skipping the sex lives of the government famous in my dispatches. Nor have I ever been persuaded that the reader was betrayed or the world endangered by letting these birds have a little privacy. . . .
>
> It is now said that details about the vices of politicians must be told to all humanity so that the public can make vitally important judgments about their "character." I doubt it. It has never been clear to me that the sexual adventurings of Franklin Roosevelt, John Kennedy, and Martin Luther King affected the creation of the New Deal, the conduct of World War II and the Cuban missile crisis, or the progress of the Civil Rights movement. Quite possibly, I suspect, had this stuff been known at the time, the principals would have been so tied up by lawyers that the Nazis would have won the war, the Soviet Union would have blown up the world, and slavery would now be making a comeback.

Sexual standards are indeed important, as we have reiterated throughout this book, but journalists must also have a sense of proportion. They must seek to avoid distortion.

In particular, it is almost always a distortion to portray flaws as if they were the total truth. That is especially evident in coverage of the presidential crisis. Yes, Bill Clinton misbehaved—badly. But does his misbehavior, endlessly exposed to view, constitute the whole truth about this man? I believe not.

Truth is much deeper and richer. It is much more elusive than the pursuit of selected facts because the truth requires judgment, on the part of both the readers or hearers and the journalists who serve them.

One of my favorite biblical texts, from the Gospel of John, reads, "You will know the truth and the truth will make you free." That, interestingly enough, is in the same chapter (chapter 8) as the story of the woman caught in adultery. The "truth" to the Christian is the truth about God, as revealed deeply in Jesus Christ. The "truth," at its deepest level, is that God is love. Applied to human beings, the "truth" is never just the sins and imperfections. It is always the deeper truth that despite everything else, here is one whom God has not rejected. There is always something more about us in our humanness than a mere recital of facts, especially just the bad ones, can possibly convey.

How does one apply this to the media? Certainly not by expecting the media to treat Christian doctrine in a privileged way. Certainly not by asking the media to refrain from exposing flaws and evildoing in various ways. But the media must accept a broader responsibility to the whole truth. The media must be conscious that they are helping to form a whole picture in the minds of people, and they cannot duck accountability when that whole picture is severely distorted and misrepresents the truth.

I am especially concerned about what happens when people are turned into abstractions or stereotypes. Because we have watched and lived with President Clinton for six years, we have a broader picture of the president and his family. This is one of the reasons why the public so persistently refuses to be trapped into defining the president only on on the basis of the flaws. That is not so true of others: the Monica Lewinskys, the Linda Tripps, the White House staffers, the congressional figures, Kenneth Starr. It is too easy to caricature these people. The truth is that they are all complex persons.

The whole *deep* truth, from the Christian perspective that I embrace, is that they are all children of God who must be loved—before they are criticized and after they are criticized.

— 6 —

The Public and Private Lives of Political Leaders

What is the relationship between public responsibility and private life? By taking on public leadership roles, do politicians give up claims to a private life? And must they? The president raised the issue himself in his August 17 statement to the nation, when he said,

> Now, this matter is between me, the two people I love most—my wife and our daughter—and our God. I must put it right, and I am prepared to do whatever it takes to do so. Nothing is more important to me personally. But it is private, and I intend to reclaim my family life for my family. It's nobody's business but ours. Even presidents have private lives.

Drawing the distinction even more forcefully, he added, "It is time to stop the pursuit of personal destruction and the prying into private lives and get on with our national life."

Public opinion polls suggest that large numbers of people agree with the president's general feelings about privacy as well as his belief that his privacy has been invaded and that, so long as the public business is attended to, the private lives of leaders should be respected. Many others, however, have declared that when one signs on to a position of highly visible leadership one must accept that one's whole life is public.

Surely the truth of the matter is that even public officials must have some privacy. And it is also true that the private lives of officials are legitimately of interest to the public. The problem is how to determine the proper *mix* of public and private spheres in the lives of leaders. There are things in the private lives of officials that most of us do not want to know and have a right to be spared knowledge of. Still, everything about a person—beliefs, actions, relationships—reflects that person's character and affects his or her leadership in one way or another. Moral character is very important, but we are often unclear about why it is important and how it is expressed.

THE CHARACTER
OF THE LEADER

I believe that the question of "character" as it involves public figures is much larger and more complicated than we usually understand it to be. Character is not just about sexual purity or even honesty, important as those virtues are. A person can be sexually above reproach and still be a scoundrel. It is even possible to be perfectly honest, at least on all factual matters, while remaining spiritually brutal. Character ultimately is about love. But clearly more must be said about this.

Some months ago, a Christian ethicist remarked that the life of a public leader is like a seamless garment, all pieces smoothly joined. There is an "interconnectedness" to it. She argued that it is not possible to separate personal character from the leader's more public positions and actions. If the personal character of a leader is flawed, then everything about that leader will be flawed, including his or her very leadership.

That view is persuasive, up to a point. It is undeniably true that personal character at least affects or influences everything a person does. A profoundly selfish person, for example, is likely to exert leadership in ways that will damage the community. Somebody who is good to the core of his or her being is likely to seek the good in public as well as private life. And there is no question but that we are very pleased when the character and public persona of politicians are of a piece, expressing wholeness and moral integrity. The angels dance for joy when such a person appears in a position of leadership.

But ordinary life is not always quite that simple. For one thing, most of the angels are in heaven and not on earth. On earth, most people are some combination of better and worse, of sinner and saint. This means that we may expect to find some sliver of goodness in the worst people, and that even the best are, to some extent, flawed. I really believe that is so. To some, this may not appear to be good Christian doctrine, but it certainly describes most of the people in the Bible.

The practical truth is that leaders whose personal lives appear to be completely virtuous can be advocates and perpetrators of terribly mistaken policies. And people of great vision who have done important things for the good of the community sometimes are the very ones with broken personal lives. I wish this were not so. I wish there were more consistency between personal morality and public morality—as sometimes there is. But such consistency is elusive.

I still recall an acquaintance who was an important figure in the California State Senate many years ago. His personal life was blighted by alcoholism and marital discord. But he was personally responsible for visionary legislation, and during the Civil Rights period of the 1960s he was a tower of courage in the face of racism. How should he be judged? I was saddened by his personal problems even as I rejoiced over his public vision and courage. I wished that somehow the public good that he stood for could be paralleled in his personal life. I did conclude that his public vision and courage were also a part of his personal character because they reflected personal values and commitments that were deeply held and dependably expressed in action.

Then there was a southern member of the U.S. Senate during that same period whose personal life was, at least as far as anybody could see, quite impeccable. He was a good family man and an active participant in his church; indeed, he was a Methodist Sunday school teacher. To the casual observer, he would be rated highly on the personal character scale, as that is generally computed. But he was in a number of ways without vision or courage. In the same Civil Rights era he was a rock-ribbed supporter of racial segregation—and that means he supported gross injustices inflicted upon people because of the color of their skin. He joined with other southern senators in a manifesto proclaiming resistance to school integration and in other ways supported a racial system that can only be described as evil. Again, it would be wonderful if the personal life of such a person could have been reflected in similar public values. But it was not to be. No doubt, his public persona was also a part of his personal character. It would have been inaccurate to judge him by the conventional signs of personal morality alone. We would have to overlook his lack of personal commitment to the clear demands of justice and his failure to be compassionate toward millions of oppressed human beings.

John Bennett, one of the great moral theologians of the twentieth century, reflected in 1958 on this issue of public and private morality from the perspective of a voting citizen, writing:

> [It is a] major error to stress the personal character or piety of a candidate without taking into account the forces which support him or the wisdom of his policies. The personal character of our leaders in public life is of great importance, but the primary emphasis should be placed upon integrity in the discharge of public responsibilities. The error appears when the private character or religious habits of a candidate become a front for interests and policies which are not examined.

Bennett observed that while morality is very important

in politics, "neither personal virtue nor sincere piety are any guarantee of social wisdom."

I believe Bennett is entirely right about this, although I want to make the further point that "social wisdom" and "integrity in the discharge of public responsibilities" are also aspects of personal character. That a Sunday school-teaching senator supports the evils of racial segregation may tell us more about his personal character than the Sunday school teaching does! So what and how are we to think about virtue, or the lack of it, in the life of a public servant? One should not conclude that moral flaws simply cancel out qualities of moral excellence. Nobody should be defined by his or her imperfections alone. I suppose it is not possible to define a person by their virtues alone, either, since we all have both virtues and imperfections.

VIRTUE IN PUBLIC LIFE

What is a virtue? The simplest traditional definition is that it is a quality of moral excellence or goodness. A virtuous person is quite simply a good person. Saint Thomas Aquinas, in the thirteenth century, defined "virtue" as a disposition of the will toward a good end. This is closely akin to the simple idea of having good habits. Virtuous people are those who habitually do good things by reflex, without having to think much about it. We have all known people like that, who when they see somebody else in need or a situation that needs remedying, just automatically respond. They are even a bit embarrassed when praised; to them, the good action is as natural as breathing. In a sense, virtues are expressed in action; but first they are indelibly present in our character. Thomas Aquinas's definition, focusing as it does upon our readiness to do good things, should not lead us to forget that there are attitudes that can be called virtuous as well. Indeed, our readiness to do good generally means that we have an attitude that leads us in that direction.

Over the course of history, many different moral qualities have been discussed and offered as virtues. Such virtues have been held out as models of moral attitude and behavior. The classic virtues of Greek philosophy included temperance (control of the passions that make us want to act against reason), fortitude (resisting the tendency to turn away from the good because of fear of toil or danger), and prudence (the ordering of the will by the mind for the sake of truth and the well-ordered life). Thomas Aquinas, who adapted these from Aristotle, added to this list the "theological" virtues of faith, hope, and love (taken from 1 Corinthians 13). The moral life is not, of course, just the sum total of such "qualities of excellence," but such time-honored virtues are suggestive. And speaking personally, out of early influences in my own moral development, I still honor the list of virtues of a Boy Scout that I committed to memory many years ago: "A Scout is trustworthy, loyal, helpful, friendly, courteous, kind, obedient, cheerful, thrifty, brave, clean, and reverent." The history of moral thought is replete with such efforts to identify such lists of moral dispositions. No list can be taken as complete, though, because the moral life is an ongoing history of human experience, in which the value of particular qualities is learned.

So living the moral life is more than the sum total of such virtues. They are a distillation from a wealth of learning, often very useful but never complete. One does not single out such qualities of life as instruments of precision, but they are usually pointers in the right direction. I say "usually," because virtues can be misapplied or carried to extremes—even when intentions are good. In fact, some virtues, taken in the wrong spirit, actually turn into vices. Thrift, for example, can become stinginess, and loyalty can become blind support of one's own group at the expense of others. Nevertheless, moral character includes the kinds of attributes we mean when we speak of virtues.

But how are we to apply the term "virtue" to public life and its leaders? There must be a relationship between personal virtues (loyalty, honesty, and kindness, for example) and the public demeanor of a leader. There must be a clear public dimension to the way the personal virtue is expressed. It may be easier to grasp this point when we see how personal virtue, when misapplied, can weaken a leader's commitment to public responsibility. Loyalty, for example, is normally a highly commendable virtue. But when a politician is loyal only to his or her friends (or cronies, we might say), that can get in the way of loyalty to the whole community. Or kindness, also a much admired virtue, can be expressed in such a way that an official responds only to the individual cases of suffering or injustice that he or she happens to encounter, meanwhile neglecting policies that might alleviate the suffering and end the injustices experienced by tens of thousands of other people whom he or she never meets personally.

But that does not mean that there is no such thing as virtue in public life. Indeed, I am fascinated by how many of the traditional "personal" virtues can be translated into highly relevant qualities of public morality. About a decade ago, I wrote on how some of the classical virtues are embodied in leaders of high character. Writing gave me the occasion to think in some ways about how helpful those old concepts of virtue can be when applied to public life. I focused on 1 Corinthians 13, the apostle Paul's eloquent description of love, which suggests that far from being nothing more than a sentimental feeling, love is specifically relevant to public attitudes and actions. Paul clearly identifies virtues that operate in the service of a harmonious community, and he grounds them in love. Here are some examples:

• **Love is patient.** Those who hope to accomplish things in public life must be in it for the long haul. The virtue of patience is found in the public attitude that sets long-term goals and takes the time necessary to fulfill them. Patience also means a willingness to put up with the smallness of people who do not share the same vision or are simply not as gifted, the willingness to take the time to clarify and share ideas and encourage people in their questioning.

• **Love is kind.** Kindness helps ease the way for the mutual accommodation of conflicting objectives, even in the face of the most serious conflict. But even when such accommodation is not possible, kindness can dissipate bitterness in the political arena, so that even adversaries recognize their fellow humanity and their common commitment to maintaining a community.

• **Love is not envious or boastful or arrogant or rude.** Put positively, love is generous, humble, and considerate. A person who has such qualities is certainly easier to get along with—and that, too, makes it easier to maintain a harmonious community. I am struck by how often disputes, even at high levels of government, are fueled by ego needs that have run out of control. A humble and generous spirit can help everybody focus on the real issues and not be preoccupied by self-centeredness.

• **Love does not insist on its own way.** In a democratic society, and possibly in *any* society, a willingness to compromise is a fundamental virtue for leaders. When leaders take an "all or nothing" attitude—or insist on winning at every point—the heaviest price we pay is a fracturing of the community that poisons the atmosphere by polarizing the society into warring camps. There are times, I suppose, when love *must* "insist on its own way," for instance to protect the poor, stop hate crimes, or preserve basic rights. But love includes the willingness to see that one's own way is not necessarily the only way to see things. Even when absolutely convinced that our "own way" is the right way, we do well to leave space for those who simply do not see it as we do.

• **Love does not rejoice in wrongdoing, but rejoices in the truth.** This statement may be especially applicable in a polarized political climate. What does it have to say about the character of those in public life who seem delighted to find flaws in the lives of their opponents, the exposure of which will ruin them? The spirit Paul commends here is rather to be *grieved* by wrongdoing, and certainly not to exaggerate it. And of course when Paul speaks of rejoicing in the truth, he is speaking not about rejoicing in facts for their own sake, but rejoicing about the deeper truth (the heart of which is love and the good of the community as God intends it).

• **Love bears all things, believes all things, hopes all things, endures all things.** Here, Paul pays tribute to endurance and fortitude. We must be willing to take a lot of abuse for the sake of the good we hope to achieve. And we are to be optimistic about the possibilities. People who have lost hope tend to become cynical—continuing to play the game of politics, but only for self-centered motives—or they may give up altogether. But love has a way of illuminating the broader possibilities, partly because love has its grounding in the God who is the source of all possibilities, but also because when we love other people we see potential there that they may not see themselves. The Civil Rights movement was intensely political, seeking objectives of the utmost importance and struggling against seemingly insurmountable laws, customs, and prejudices. But it was infused throughout with a spirit of love, not only for those whose liberation was its primary objective, but also for its adversaries. That spirit of love helped Civil Rights activists see the possibilities for change in attitudes and institutions.

Even from this brief discussion, we can see that love is central to all of life. It is at the heart of all moral character and virtue. Moreover, love is specifically relevant to public life precisely because it is so *constructive*. A political leader of high character is one who, most of all, is dedicated to leaving the world a better place. She or he cannot possibly know all those who will be affected by her or his leadership personally. But still, the soul of such a person is full of love for those who will be affected.

A virtuous public figure cannot be content with mere enjoyment of the political game and of playing it well. It is much more than seeking office for the sake of what one imagines one will *be;* it means seeking office for the sake of the good that one can *do.* Therefore, a politician of high character is prepared to lose, if need be, for the sake of the good. At least, such a leader has some notion of the battles that are worth "dying" in, if need be.

As an illustration of that, I have long been an admirer of the late Brooks Hays, a member of Congress from Arkansas for many years. A progressive politician, Hays was also a religious leader, serving for a time as president of his denomination, the Southern Baptist Convention. When the issue of racial segregation came to a head in 1958, Central High School of Little Rock, Arkansas, became an important battleground. Hays was placed under great pressure to support continued racial segregation, but that was where he felt he had to draw the line. He simply would not be a part of the effort to resist desegregation. As a result, he lost the next election to an unknown write-in candidate who surfaced at the last minute. I heard the former congressman speak of this a couple of times, with rueful humor but never with the slightest hint that he had not done the right thing. That was, I thought, real *character* in a politician.

Former senator Mark Hatfield wrote an instructive book on the dilemmas of morality in politics, aptly titled *Between a Rock and a Hard Place*. Among his many wise observations is his portrait of the conflict within the soul of the politician between "the allurement of power and honor" and the recognition that "service to others, solely for their own behalf and even entailing deep sacrifice, is the true essence of leadership." That goal of service is, he feels, "the ultimate form of power." When he came to this realization in his own life, Hatfield reports, he felt newly liberated "from the idolatry of power and given over more deeply to a whole new vision of prophetic witness, faithfulness, and servanthood."

It is very important that we understand that the question of "character" in public figures is so much larger than we usually understand it to be. As we have said, character is not just about sexual purity or even honesty, important as those virtues are. It is about love, in the grandest possible sense of that word. In evaluating the character of public figures we must recognize their personal flaws, but much more than that we must test our leaders' commitment to the public good and willingness to sacrifice for that good.

A President as a Moral Leader

In the midst of the crisis, I found myself one day in a public discussion with the Reverend Jerry Falwell. He and

I were not exactly on the same page, as the saying goes, and our conversation was spirited. In the course of the interview he remarked, as he had frequently in other venues, that the president should resign. That did not surprise me, since he had opposed President Clinton even before the president's first election. He announced that he bore the president no ill will and that we should, in fact, forgive him for his actions, but he argued that the president, by his actions, had disqualified himself for the nation's highest office.

To drive the point home, Falwell compared Clinton's sexual misbehavior to that of some clergypersons of his acquaintance who had similarly fallen from grace. In those cases, he reported, the ministers were forgiven and their healing was facilitated, but they had to leave their pulpits.

I was fascinated by the analogy, and even tempted by it. Should we not hold the president of the United States to an even higher standard than that imposed upon a parish minister? And what about the military, in which a number of officers have been cashiered for the sexual harassment of subordinates?

There is enough truth in these analogies to consider the president's misbehavior to be of more than trivial importance. He did set a bad example for the nation. His sexual activity was carried out in a context of large discrepancies of age, power, and position—even though it appears that there was no pressure ever brought to bear on Ms. Lewinsky. Nonetheless, there remains the question of the president's moral leadership. Should he not as Reverend Falwell suggested, be held to as high a standard as a minister— or even higher?

This really is a more complex question than it appears to be on the surface. Part of the complexity is reflected in the argument one could hear frequently in those "man on the street" interviews during the time of crisis: "We didn't elect President Clinton to be a priest or minister. We elected him to be the chief executive. As long as he is doing that job, what he does in his private life should be of no concern to us." Is that a legitimate argument?

It is at least true that, unlike a pastor, priest, or rabbi, the president is not *primarily* a moral leader. The contrast is especially apparent when a religious leader exploits the trust of people who are turning to him or her for spiritual guidance in a time of their own vulnerability. Then, one might say, the very essence of the leader's office has been violated. That is arguably also the case when, in the military chain of command, a higher officer exploits a subordinate. That fundamentally affects unit morale and cohesion.

Of course, while a president's role, compared to these examples, is somewhat different, there is no question that a president is in a position to exert moral influence and that his behavior affects the perceptions of others. That, no doubt, was one of the reasons for the attempted cover-up. It is doubtful whether there was any element of coercion even implied in the relationship.

But there is a deeper issue of moral leadership that strangely has not been much noted by the pundits. When it became evident that Ms. Lewinsky was more than willing to be a part of this misbehavior, the president at that moment had an opportunity to help her to become more mature, to grow morally. A standard principle in pastoral counseling is that if the person who is being counseled makes a sexual advance, the pastor, in refusing to participate can help him or her see and deal with psychological issues giving rise to this behavior pattern. The question in such a situation is whether the person being counseled will be further enmeshed in a harmful spiritual state or, instead, be helped to grow out of it. Of course, presidents are not generally trained as counselors; nor are they expected to play that role. But there remains enough similarity in the situation to feel that an important opportunity for moral leadership was lost, and with sad consequences.

So, back to Jerry Falwell's question, should the president—like the clergypersons to whom Falwell referred—be forgiven and extended help with the healing process but still be removed from office? I don't believe so, as the following chapter will make clear. But in direct response to Reverend Falwell, I'm not sure I would always insist on that for the clergy either. The question should be whether the person has lost the ability to function effectively in the office and if healing is possible. In some cases, such as clergy who have been involved in child sexual abuse, the consensus among professionals is that it is a mistake for such a person ever again to have access to children in the way that clergy do. Apart from that, there are numerous illustrations of clergy who have fallen from grace and then been restored, sometimes to a much more effective ministry than ever before. The misbehavior is not winked at and passed by, but neither is it treated as a fatal disease. Often, as in the case with the president, the offending clergy have important gifts for their calling that should not be wasted. Sometimes, the very fact that the clergyperson has gone through such a personal experience of brokenness makes him or her even more sensitive to the brokenness of others—although that would hardly be a good reason for clergy to do the things that contribute to brokenness.

I am not as familiar with the problems of the military, although I am aware of some of the more highly publicized cases. Some of the publicized military sex scandals have clearly involved harassment, while others seem to have had to do with more consensual relationships. In most of the publicized cases, some form of discipline was clearly needed to mark the behavior off as unacceptable. I am not so sure that removal is always necessary. Very gifted military officers, some with many years of training and experience behind them, can still make important contributions to their service and the nation—provided they will receive the right kind of remediation and provided the unmistakable message they receive is that sexual misconduct is unacceptable. When our attitude toward these situations is truly grounded in love, we will always look for the least destructive, most constructive solutions.

But beyond these questions related to moral leadership, there is another way in which the role of a president is different from a pastor's or a military officer's role. The president not only has a particular job, he or she is also the instrument of an important political decision made by the people. The president is at the heart of a configuration of power and policy, an expression of the democratically determined will of the nation. The removal of a president is therefore an act of enormous gravity. The gravity is further suggested by the constitutional language governing impeachment, that it shall be reserved for "high crimes and misdemeanors." While not further defined, the word "high" suggests impeachment should not be for small or even moderate forms of misbehavior. I will return to this question in the concluding chapter, but I wish to repeat here that even though a president's office is categorically different from other jobs or positions in society, that does not take away the wrongfulness of misbehavior.

Nor does the position of the presidency eliminate the importance of moral leadership in that office. But given the special role of a president as chief of state (and as an expression of the will of the people), the *form* of moral leadership required of a president is also broadly different from that required of a religious leader. The president's moral responsibility is to support and articulate the fundamental values of the nation. For instance, the president is responsible for interpreting and defending the human rights of all members of the society, even those who may have voted for a different candidate or who didn't or couldn't vote at all. Thus, in our time, a president continues to exercise moral leadership in reminding everybody of the humanity of people who are being neglected and in challenging the realities of racism and of hate groups in our society. A president acts and speaks in defense of the public health and safety. A president, in moments of tragedy or catastrophe, serves to articulate the grief and fellow feeling of the whole community. A president reminds the nation of its world responsibilities, both for the sake of the "national interest" and in recognition that the human values of the people of one society are enhanced by recognition of those of other societies as well. These are very important, even indispensable, forms of moral leadership by a president of the United States.

In a word, a president is a moral leader precisely as he or she articulates, defends, supports, and enhances the deeper values of the nation as a whole.

The ability of anybody to do that is, of course, quite limited. Some presidents have been much better than others. Some have been put to the test, through war or economic hardship, more than others. All of our presidents, every single one of them, have been flawed. But all of our presidents have also had at least this in common: Their accession to the office of president has been an expression of the will of the people, either through direct election or through constitutional provision for succession. Thus, there is both a special expectation by the people that their president will lead and a willingness by the people to accept that leadership, including moral leadership of the sort I have suggested and as leadership of a more practical sort.

The special responsibilities embodied in the holder of that office should therefore be set aside only with fear and trembling, and only with evidence of a clear abandonment of the public good. We want a public leader to exemplify high standards, both of private and public moral behavior. In both, love should be the central point of focus. But our primary emphasis in evaluating national leaders is their demonstrated love of the people and nation they serve.

— 7 —

The Way Out

As I think about the situation we face, I turn to the Bible and, at this moment, especially to Psalm 40:

> I waited patiently for the Lord; he inclined to me and heard my cry. He drew me up from the desolate pit, out of the miry bog, and set my feet upon a rock, making my steps secure. He put a new song in my mouth. . . . Be pleased, O Lord, to deliver me; O Lord make haste to help me. (vv. 1–3, 13)

It certainly does seem like a "miry bog" we are in! How can we get out of this morass without further damage to the nation? Who or what will deliver us? The Psalm begins with great confidence, but as it proceeds the Psalmist wavers between confidence in God and pleas to God. Even the ending expresses that tension: "You are my help and my deliverer," the Psalmist says with confidence. But then the plea, "Do not delay, O my God." That must be the plea of many people who find themselves in the middle of such a "miry bog."

OUR SELF-UNDERSTANDING
AS A PEOPLE

I suggested earlier that in this national crisis, it is our self-understanding that has been at stake. On September 11, the day of the White House prayer breakfast, two alternative paths were set in front of the American people. One was the path of the prayer breakfast, with its tone of repentance, forgiveness, love, restoration, and healing. The other was the path of the Starr Report, with its emphasis upon exposing sins and crimes and passing judgment.

Which of these represents the more promising way to define our meaning as a nation? We must resolve the issue of how we are to understand ourselves as a people before we can ask what we are to do. The one flows from the other.

If, on the one hand, we are to define ourselves, at the most fundamental level, as a nation of laws, the overriding national issue becomes simply whether or not the laws are obeyed. In a legalistic spirit we might take the Starr Report at face value and, if we believe its allegations, say: The president has disobeyed laws, especially those pertaining to lying under oath. As president, he is responsible for upholding and protecting the law. By violating the law he has forfeited any claim upon the office, and so he must be removed either through forced resignation or impeachment. If the law, as law, is what is important, it does not even matter how serious the law or the circumstance of its violation. If a nation tolerates the violation of the law by its chief executive, it abrogates our self-definition as a nation of laws.

The Starr Report also lays out numerous illustrations of presidential sin, in some detail. Sin and crime are not exactly the same thing. There are some behaviors that may be immoral but not illegal. But sin is contrary to moral teaching. And if we understand ourselves as a nation of law, that could be understood to include a moral code as well. Under this understanding of our national identity, it could also be intolerable for the chief executive, as the nation's chief moral teacher, to violate the moral code. Taking note of such things, some have defined the presidential misconduct as "conduct unbecoming a president" and have treated this, in itself, as sufficient grounds for removal from office.

The assumption here is that in a society governed by law and moral codes, one upholds the law by enforcing it. To let somebody "get away with" violating the law and immorality weakens the law and moral standards. That is especially so in the case of the president. In a nation of laws, it is important to establish the principle that nobody is above the law, not even the president. Or, one might say, especially not the president, since the president is not only chief executive but chief example.

I do not wonder that some people consider this so obvious that they cannot begin to understand why anybody would disagree. To them, the case for the removal of the president from office is incontestably clear. Their moral rhetoric can soar on the wings of high principle and the majesty of law. To their way of thinking, law represents the heart and soul of the nation's life. That is one way to define the nation, and the Starr Report appeals to and confirms this state of mind.

The other path to resolution was suggested by the spirit of the White House prayer breakfast. From this perspective, we are a society that should understand itself more deeply as a community of love than as a community of law. To be sure, love and law are not necessarily inconsistent or incompatible. But it matters, perhaps a whole lot, which of the two is understood to be the foundation of our life together as a people. If law comes first, then love is subordinated. If love comes first, then law is there to serve community. I have the impression that some, in their eagerness to remove this president from office, would do that in conformity with their conception of law, even if it tore the community apart. Those who place a higher premium upon community and love can still take law and moral standards very seriously, but they feel that the spirit of legalism is at odds with community and love.

It should be no secret now that I am among those who place the greater emphasis upon community and love. In this, I believe I am in harmony with the apostle Paul's emphasis upon grace. "Grace" is love and forgiveness that we receive even when we do not deserve it. There are different interpretations of this in Christian theology. But Paul understood that we are all sinners who stand in need of love from God. As we receive God's love, in a trusting spirit, we recognize that we have no basis for self-righteousness. That is why, when questioned by a television moderator about the president's "character," I had to reply that even though I had not done the things of which he was accused, I still could not say to him, "Bill Clinton, I am a better man than you are." Who is to say that his or her form of sin is less serious than that of another person, whose behavior may be more highly publicized? Indeed, the spirit of self-righteousness may itself be the deeper form of sin. Our primary interest should not be in judging and condemning others whom we consider to be worse than ourselves; rather, our focus should be on reconciliation, healing, and restoration. Above all, we want ours to be a community of mutual caring and public spiritedness. No community on earth can perfectly exemplify this. But true morality is grounded in such love, and that is the direction in which we can seek to go.

What, then, about the law? If law is not the ultimate foundation of community life, it is still necessary. Laws can give effect to a society's developing conception of what is good. A good case can be made for many, if not most, laws on the books. For instance, laws banning racial discrimination and laws requiring honesty in the courtroom have a very solid rationale behind them. They are not, in general, opposed to love but are in the service of love. If they are not obeyed for the sake of something deeper, however, than that they are laws to be obeyed, then they do not reflect a very deep morality. Another way to say this is that law defines minimum standards of behavior, below which deviation will be punished. True morality rises above the minimum expectations of behavior to express common purpose and mutual caring.

The spirit of the prayer breakfast took those minimums into account. That was why the participants felt that repentance was appropriate, even necessary. But the spirit of the prayer breakfast went far beyond the recognition of minimum standards of behavior to encompass forgiveness, reconciliation, and love, which are never "the minimum." It was finally a very constructive spirit.

Is a society such as ours capable of forgiveness, reconciliation, and love? God help us if we are not! For if we are not, then most of the religious traditions of this country are nothing but sentimentality. How can we worship a God of love in church or synagogue, then turn around and deny the applicability of love to the life of the wider community? Is that not hypocrisy? On the other hand, if we find ways to affirm love in the wider community, then our various religious institutions and communities of faith will have a much more secure foundation. All of us, including those who are not a part of any religious group, have a great stake in the definition of the nation rooted in love. It is only in such a nation that the rich diversity of its peoples can be affirmed, not merely tolerated. Only in such a nation will the most vulnerable of its people be accepted and protected. Only in such a nation can we be sure that we, in our own moments of vulnerability, will be a matter of community concern. Only in such a nation can we hope to find restoration and wholeness when in some aspects of our lives we have lost our way.

TOWARD A
CONSTRUCTIVE SOLUTION

The presenting issue through most of the crisis has been the question, How do we as a country respond to the president's actions?

Those who define the situation legalistically, as we have seen, want him out of office. Some lace their language with words of condemnation, and their spirit is harshly punitive. They might be generous enough to not have the president prosecuted criminally after he leaves office—if he goes quickly and voluntarily. Others are more forgiving at the personal level but feel that he has forfeited the office and must be forced out, one way or another. They will wish him well afterward. Some believe sincerely that he cannot get on with his personal healing as long as he has the pressure of office. To them, it is a kindness to see to his removal.

I disagree with all of this. No doubt, it would be a genuine relief to the president to be spared the incessant pressures of a hostile prosecutor and Congress, not to mention a fair portion of the nation's press. But I cannot imagine that leaving office under these circumstances would actually contribute to his own healing process, for the burden of remorse would be so greatly enlarged.

But apart from Bill Clinton's personal life, I am very concerned about the effect that his forced removal would have upon the nation. If it is widely believed—and it would be—that he had been hounded from office by longtime political adversaries, the poison in the political atmosphere would taint government and the political system long into the future. The United States is far removed geographically and politically from those trouble spots in the world where endless cycles of vindictive retribution have made civil politics nearly impossible. And I do not believe the forced removal of President Clinton would cause armed conflict and terrorism. But the spirit engendered by it might be similar, as millions of people found that the president they had elected had been removed for what they perceived to be relatively trivial reasons. Trivial? To be sure, perjury (by some accounts the strongest case against him) is not in itself trivial. But if it has been committed in a civil proceeding, in a case subsequently thrown out, and where there is even some, admittedly hairsplitting, possibility of defense, then one can argue that it is relatively trivial. Even the subsequent charges of perjury all stem from the effort to hush up a sex scandal, not from some weighty matter of state. Unquestionably many people disagree with that line of analysis, but I believe that the president's forced removal from office would polarize society for years to come.

Removing him from office would also be a way to undermine the presidency itself, even granting that the president's own behavior has helped to do just that. If behavior that no one could reasonably characterize as a "high crime and misdemeanor" is used to remove a president, we will have come a long way toward routinely using special prosecutors and impeachment proceedings as a weapon of political warfare. Does our nation really want that? If it is important that the president be punished in some fashion, do we at the same time want to reward the way the special prosecutor has gone about *his* work—including using information derived from surreptitiously (and possibly illegally) tape-recorded conversations of friends, invading lawyer-client privilege, and intruding into the president's Secret Service protectors?

Still, as we are reminded by the president's critics, illegality and misbehavior must have consequences. If a president can "get away with" such conduct, the nation's standards of righteousness and law observance are inevitably weakened. The conduct truly was serious, and most would agree that such conduct must indeed have consequences.

Of course it already *has* had consequences! I cannot imagine any objective person looking at the events of 1998 and concluding that the president "got away with" anything. This has been an enormously painful year for him and for his family. What future president—or other politician, for that matter—could not derive from this experience the notion that such sexual misconduct and efforts at cover-up are risky in the extreme?

Still, a strong case can be made for some sort of public consequence, for the sake of current society and history. I do not believe, however, that impeachment or criminal proceedings are appropriate means. Such sanctions would be far too punitive for the character of the offense and far too damaging to the body politic. Moreover, they do not really reach the deeper issues in a culture where sex is so often separated from love and commitment.

Punitive treatment of one person is more akin to the ancient scapegoating behavior of ritually heaping the sins of the community on the one who is then driven from the community. If the heart of the problem is the disconnection between sex and love, how can we possibly heal such a moral "disease" in such an unloving way?

I believe that a better, less destructive way to register the country's will is by a formal resolution of Congress, the legislative body representing the people. Through Congress, the people can announce that this conduct has been unacceptable. While there is little precedent for this, there is no reason under heaven why Congress could not adopt such a resolution and (morally if not legally) demand the president's presence at the Capitol to hear it in person.

Former president Gerald R. Ford has called for exactly such a procedure. He was, he wrote in the *New York Times*, deeply concerned about the need to spare "the country I love from further turmoil or uncertainty." He envisioned a process in which a "harshly worded rebuke" would be "rendered by members of both parties." The event would be televised, and the president would be present to accept both the rebuke and full responsibility for his actions.

A student of medieval church history could find in this a modern-day adaptation of the penitence of King Henry IV before Pope Gregory VII. The king had defied the pope and been excommunicated as a result. To free himself of the excommunication, he stood barefoot in the snow on three successive days at the gate of a castle where the pope was residing. Henry IV recovered, presumably without frostbite.

President Ford called upon Congress to behave in a nonpartisan, generous fashion: "Let all this be done without partisan exploitation or mean-spiritedness." The election returns of 1998 suggest that that is really what the country continues to want the Congress to do.

CAN MORAL AUTHORITY AND TRUST BE RESTORED?

It is difficult to conceive of real healing occurring on any other kind of basis. Nonetheless, one must ask whether the president's moral authority and trust can truly be restored. There is so much cynicism in the land in this year of crisis! So many people, no matter what they believe about the case at hand, have lost trust in the integrity of the nation's institutions and leadership. That is a sad thing. Democracy lays heavy demands upon us, above all the need to trust one another and to feel confident that those who have been elected to office can be trusted to serve faithfully. Some have said that regardless of what is done, President Clinton has forever lost his moral authority and his ability to be trusted by the people.

Such a gloomy assessment is not warranted. A "cleansing" moment, such as President Ford has advocated, would not be very pleasant for anybody, least of all for the president himself. But it really could clear the air. The proposed process reminds me a bit of the interventions that are sometimes arranged for alcoholics or drug addicts. Typically, friends and loved ones will gather in a room. The addict will be brought there, usually unsuspectingly, and confronted by those nearest and dearest to him with his behavior. Concrete measures for reform will be laid out in such a way that the addict will have little alternative but to cooperate. It is "tough love," but with genuine emphasis upon "love." Is such a person, having been humbled in that way, ever to regain the moral esteem and trust of the participants? Of course! The intent of this is restoration, not vindictiveness or destructiveness.

I believe the country wants to restore the leadership of this president, partly for the sake of the institution of the presidency but also for the sake of a person who is still greatly appreciated even despite his flaws.

Many Americans believe Bill Clinton has been a good president, a fine leader. Many things have gone well on his "watch." He has been gifted in the arts of reconciliation, and he has grown immensely in his grasp of the problems of the nation and the world. Such gifts are not to be squandered, either by him or by the nation. Among his gifts has been a striking resiliency. He has, in his political career, suffered serious setbacks, but he has always recovered with grace and good humor.

I believe his resiliency has spiritual roots. I can imagine that, after a "cleansing" event such as President Ford has proposed, he would take up his tasks with renewed enthusiasm and with response from an appreciative people. I have been impressed by his ability, even under the trying circumstances of this year, to give effective service in a number of important areas. That ability could only be enhanced because the cloud would be lifted.

Personal Healing

In his statement to the religious leaders at the prayer breakfast, the president acknowledged his need for personal healing and his commitment to change. I have been asked whether that change is possible for him—even if that is really his intention. My answer to both questions is, emphatically, Yes. The process of change can be very difficult, sometimes because the flaws in our character have roots of which we are not fully conscious. Understanding better the sources of one's self-destructive behavior can be very liberating. I believe in this with all my heart.

Pastors, in common with therapists and the various twelve-step programs, are in the business of change. I could not function very long as a pastor if I did not believe that hurt people can be healed and broken lives restored.

Can Bill Clinton get on with the mending and the changing even while carrying the immense burdens of the presidency? In answer to that, we can note that whatever the sources of his flawed behavior, the president has managed to carry out his responsibilities in a very effective manner. That is partly because he is genuinely committed to doing so. It is also because there is much in his life and character that is *not* flawed. Throughout his political career, he has embodied many of the virtues of public leadership I noted in chapter 6 and many of the more private virtues as well. I find him to be a genuinely caring person and one uniquely fitted to combining the spiritual gifts of love with the intellectual gifts of competence. I do not want to overstate any of this. But let us not understate it either.

One thing more must be added concerning the president's healing process and our own as well. In the midst of the sin and the tragedy of this national crisis, there is nothing that will help him and us more than a genuine rebirth of compassion. People need moral standards and corrective criticism, but none of that helps much if it does not rest upon compassion. How often, as a pastor, I have seen that when people genuinely experience love they are able to find liberation from the troubled parts of their lives. I have suggested, in these pages, that the root of our problems are in the disconnections between life and love. I have spoken of the gulf between sex and loving commitment, pervasive in our culture, sometimes highly visible in individual persons. We can also speak of the disconnections between politics and love, or law and love, or economics and love. The moral corruptions and cynicisms at work in our nation are a product of such disconnection.

But our nation, like its president, already has great reservoirs of spiritual strength from which to work. At our best we are a people of compassion and public spiritedness, despite our individual moments of meanness. Our opportunity and challenge now is to use those strengths in dealing with our weaknesses. We will all be the better for it.

As I draw this book to an end, my mind returns to those late summer days by the peaceful lake in the Adirondacks to which I referred in the first chapter. Amidst the natural beauty of the mountains and especially as I gazed at the night sky, it was easier to see things in perspective. I remember a little song we sang in the church camps of my youth, in the mountains of Arizona.

> Evening skies! Sunrise! Lakes and rushing water;
> Make all things unlovely from my soul depart . . .
> Starry skies! Moonrise! Far, eternal heavens;
> Take away my smallness, Make me long to grow.

This is my prayer for our nation: Dear God, take away our smallness! Make us long to grow!